Why Effort Fails

 **Field & Frame Press**
Works in Applied Philosophy of Human Systems

Why Effort Fails

(It's Not What You Think)

James Zboran

Why Effort Fails: (It's Not What You Think)

First edition, 2026

ISBN 978-0-9844331-9-3 (paperback)

Library of Congress Control Number: 2026906867

Publisher's imprint:

Field & Frame Press
Works in Applied Philosophy of Human Systems

Published by Jim Zboran Group
Rolla, Missouri
www.jimzborangroup.com

Printed in the United States of America

10 9 8 7 6 5 4 3 2 1

Applied Philosophy of Human Systems™ and APHS™ are trademarks of James Zboran.

Table of Contents

A Note to the Reader

This book comes out of a field.

The field is called Applied Philosophy of Human Systems. It is a structured inquiry into how human beings function as self-organizing systems within their lives: how they get stuck, how they move, and what the difference between those two states actually consists of. Its founding papers are available for those who want the complete architecture. Its companion monograph, included here as Appendix A, maps that architecture in full. Neither is required to make use of what follows. This book was written to stand on its own.

What it means that this book comes out of a field is simply this: the ideas in it were not assembled from observation alone. They were developed systematically, tested against each other for coherence, and refined over time. The language used here (frame, self-organizing system, orientation, protective choosing) carries specific meanings developed through that process. Where those terms appear, they are doing precise work. Reading them as roughly equivalent to their everyday use will occasionally be accurate. Reading them as having been chosen carefully will more often serve you.

• • •

This is not a self-help book, though it may help.

It is not a psychology book, though it draws on the same territory. It is not a philosophy text, though the field it comes from is philosophical in its foundations. The category it fits most closely is probably this: a serious account of something people commonly experience. The gap between effort and movement. Written with the precision the subject deserves and the directness the reader has earned by having already tried the simpler explanations.

The restraint that distinguishes it from most books in adjacent territory is real and deliberate. This book does not tell you what to do. It tells you what is actually happening. The field it draws on holds that accurate understanding of where you are changes what becomes visible from there, and that visible options do not need to be prescribed. If that claim seems either too modest or too convenient, the chapters ahead will either earn your trust or they won't. The claim is tested against your own experience, not defended in advance.

• • •

The book is designed to be read in sequence.

Each chapter builds on what the previous ones have established. This is not a collection of independent ideas that can be sampled in any order; it is a cumulative argument, and the later chapters depend on the earlier ones having landed. The understanding being offered here is structural: each piece of it is held in place by the pieces around it, and removing one changes the weight the others can bear. A reader who begins at Chapter 9 will find the material harder to locate than one who arrives there through what precedes it.

This is also not a book that asks to be read quickly. The ideas are not dense in the way that requires slow parsing, but they are precise in a way that rewards attention. The experience this book is trying to change is one most readers have been inside for some time. The understanding that changes it tends to arrive not in a single moment of recognition but through a gradual shift in how familiar territory looks, a shift that each chapter is designed to move forward by a specific amount. Giving that process the time it needs is the only thing asked of you here.

The rest is the book's responsibility.

1. The Promise

What this book solves

There is a specific experience this book is written for. It is not failure in the dramatic sense. Not catastrophe, not collapse, not the kind of not-working that announces itself loudly and demands immediate attention. It is something quieter and, in its own way, harder to name.

It is the experience of having tried. Of having applied real effort, in good faith, to something that mattered, and of having arrived, after all that effort, somewhere close to where you started. Of having done what the situation seemed to call for and found that the call went unanswered. Of having worked at something long enough and seriously enough that the most available explanation (the one that arrives quietly, without being invited) is that the problem is you.

Not that you failed once. That you keep failing. That something in you resists the movement you are trying to make, in a way that looks, from close enough, like a fact about who you are.

This book is written for the person carrying that explanation. Not to reassure them that the explanation is wrong. Reassurance is not what changes this. But to replace it with a more accurate one. The reason effort fails is not personal. It is structural. And the difference between those two accounts is not a matter of comfort. It is a matter of what you can actually do about it.

• • •

The structural account is this: effort fails when it is applied at the wrong level.

Not when it is insufficient. Not when the person making it is inadequate. Not when the timing is wrong or the method is weak or the commitment is shallow. When it is located at a level that cannot reach where the problem actually lives.

The problem, in cases where effort consistently fails, lives in something this book calls a frame: an orientational structure that organizes what you perceive as possible, necessary, or constrained before you consciously interpret anything. The frame is prior to deliberate thought. It is the condition within which effort is applied. When the frame doesn't fit the actual situation, effort applied within it (no matter how disciplined, how sustained, how skillfully executed) addresses the problem as the frame has defined it, *not as the situation actually is.*

This distinction, between the problem as the frame defines it and the problem as it actually is, is the central distinction of this book. Understanding it fully is what changes the relationship to effort, to stuck, to the experience of working hard and not moving. Not because the understanding provides a new technique to apply, but because it changes where you are standing. And standing somewhere different changes what is available.

• • •

This book is written for two kinds of readers, and both of them are already in the room.

The first is the person for whom the experience described above is personal and immediate. Someone who has worked at something that matters: a relationship, a professional transition, a pattern they have been trying to change, a direction they have been trying to move in, and who has encountered the specific exhaustion that comes not from working hard but from working hard without landing anywhere. Who has tried the approaches that are generally recommended. Who has found, in each case, that something essential remained unchanged. Who has started, with some reluctance, to take that unchanged thing as evidence of something about themselves.

That reader does not need more encouragement. They do not need another framework or a better method or a more inspiring account of what is possible. They need an accurate explanation of what has actually been happening, one that locates the problem correctly, at the level where it actually lives. This book provides that explanation.

The second reader works with people who are trying hard and not moving. Coaches, therapists, consultants, teachers, leaders, managers: anyone who sits regularly across from another person in the experience of stuck and tries to help them through it. This reader may already sense that what is missing in their most difficult cases is not technique. That something upstream of technique is what determines whether the work reaches the level where it can actually connect. This book provides the structural account of what that upstream thing is.

Both readers share the same core experience, approached from different angles: the gap between effort and movement. This book explains that gap. Not as a metaphor. Not as motivation. As a structural account of what is actually happening, at the level where it is actually happening, which is the only level from which something can actually be done about it.

. . .

A word about what this book does not do, because naming it clearly is part of the promise.

This book does not prescribe action. It does not end with a plan, a practice, a set of steps, or a morning routine. There is no framework to implement and no method to apply. That restraint is explained fully in Chapter 3, but the short version belongs here: action that follows from accurate understanding does not need to be prescribed. It follows naturally. What this book provides is the understanding. What you do with it is yours.

The field this book draws on is Applied Philosophy of Human Systems. Its founding papers (three volumes, available for those who want the complete architecture) are not required reading. This book is complete without them. A companion monograph, included at the back as Appendix A, provides a full structural overview of the field for readers who want to understand the framework behind the ideas encountered here. Also not required. Also complete in itself.

What follows is twelve chapters. The first two establish what the problem is not: the usual explanations and why they reach their limit where they do. The third maps what the book actually delivers and how. Chapters 4 through 11 deliver it. Chapter 12 describes what it looks like when it has landed.

That is the complete architecture. It is organized around a single promise: by the time you finish, you will understand why effort fails, not as a general observation about human psychology, but as a precise structural account of what has been happening in your specific experience of not moving. And that understanding, arrived at fully and not just intellectually, changes something that no amount of trying could change.

That is what this book is for.

2. Why the Usual Answers Fall Short

The obstacles

Before this book can offer something different, it needs to account for what you have already tried.

Not in the spirit of dismissal. The approaches most people reach for when effort isn't working are not wrong. They are not foolish. They are not evidence of inadequate thinking or insufficient research. They represent the accumulated practical wisdom of a culture that takes the problem of stuck seriously and has produced, in good faith, its best available answers. Those answers help a great many people a great deal of the time.

But they have a ceiling. A specific one, with a specific structure. And the reader for whom this book exists has already encountered that ceiling, not once, but repeatedly, in ways that have started to feel personal. This chapter's job is to locate that ceiling precisely. Not to make you feel foolish for having pressed against it. To make visible exactly where each approach stops, and why it stops there, so that the question this book is actually answering comes into focus.

There are five approaches. Each one is worth understanding fully, because understanding what it can do makes the nature of what it cannot do clear.

. . .

The first approach is the most natural one, and the one most people reach for first: try harder.

When effort isn't producing movement, apply more of it. More discipline, more commitment, more consistency. Wake earlier, stay later, hold the line more firmly. The assumption underneath this response is so widely shared that it almost never surfaces as an assumption: the problem is insufficient effort. The person who isn't moving isn't trying hard enough. The solution, therefore, is to try harder.

This assumption is sometimes correct. There are many situations where what's missing is exactly what it appears to be: more consistent effort, applied more rigorously, over a longer time. In those situations, trying harder works. The feedback is clear and the progress, while gradual, is real.

But there is a different situation that looks nearly identical from the outside and feels, from the inside, almost indistinguishable from the first. It is the situation where effort is not insufficient but mislocated. Where the direction being pursued is not the direction that reaches the problem. Where more energy applied consistently in a particular direction produces faster movement away from where movement actually needs to go, or produces exhaustion from sustained effort that cannot connect to what it needs to reach.

In this situation, trying harder does not help. It cannot help, not because the person lacks the capacity for discipline, but because discipline applied in a mislocated direction is still mislocated.

The ceiling here is not about effort. It is about whether the effort is aimed at the level where the problem actually lives.

The reader who has tried harder, sincerely and repeatedly, and arrived back in approximately the same place, has encountered this ceiling. What it means is not that they didn't try hard enough. It means the problem is somewhere that trying harder cannot reach.

• • •

The second approach arrives when the first one fails: think differently.

This is the more sophisticated response, and it represents a genuine advance on the first. Rather than applying more energy to the same direction, it asks whether the direction itself reflects a distorted or limited way of seeing. Reframe the situation. Adopt a different perspective on the obstacle. Shift the beliefs that are keeping you stuck. Stop seeing failure as a verdict and start seeing it as information. Change the way you're thinking about this, and what's possible will change.

This approach is correct about something important. The way a situation is interpreted does shape what responses to it are visible. The person who believes they are fundamentally incapable of something will not perceive opportunities that the person without that belief would perceive. Perspective matters. Deliberate effort to see differently can be genuinely useful, and for many people in many situations, it is.

The ceiling appears at a specific point, and it's the same point for everyone who has tried this approach and found it didn't hold: deliberate reframing operates at the surface of the structure that actually organizes perception. The conscious mind can conclude that failure is information and not a verdict. It can be entirely sincere in that conclusion. And the structure beneath conscious thought (what this book will call a frame) can continue organizing experience as though failure is a verdict, because the conclusion reached at the surface of the structure did not reach the structure itself.

This is not a failure of sincerity or effort. The insight was real. The problem is architectural. Conscious thought occurs within the frame. It cannot, from that position, reliably change the frame. The person who understands this has not understood something discouraging. They have understood why the approach reached its limit at that specific point and not somewhere else.

The reader who has genuinely shifted their thinking (who reached a real insight, felt it land, held it for a week or a month) and then watched the old pattern quietly reassert itself has encountered this ceiling directly. The thinking changed. The organizing structure did not. That is not a personal failure. It is a structural property of how frames work.

• • •

When mindset work doesn't hold, the search for better technique begins.

The third approach is methodological: find the right framework, the right system, the right process. The problem, on this account, is not effort and not perspective: it's method. You have been using the wrong tool. The right one will work where the others haven't. And so the search for better technique continues: a new planning system, a different productivity framework, a more refined approach to the specific domain where the stuck keeps appearing.

This approach, too, is useful within its range. Methods are not irrelevant. Some tools are more suited to particular problems than others, and there are genuine cases where the missing piece really is a better approach to the task at hand. The person who has been managing a complex project with inadequate tools will often find that better tools make a real difference.

The ceiling here is the same as the ceiling on conscious reframing, approached from a different angle. Tools operate within frames. They are designed to address problems as those problems are defined by the existing way of seeing the situation. When the frame itself is generating the stuck (when the way the situation is being organized is what makes movement unavailable), no tool within the frame can reach that level. The tool can only address the problem as the frame has defined it. It cannot question the definition.

The reader who has tried every available method (and there are readers who have tried a great many) and still finds something essential unchanged is not encountering a limitation of their research. They are encountering the structural ceiling of methodological approaches to a problem that lives above the level methods operate at. The methods were not wrong. They were operating at the wrong level.

• • •

When methods don't produce the expected movement, the explanation often shifts: the problem must be motivational.

You have lost touch with why this matters. The connection to your purpose has weakened, the drive has dimmed, the sense of what you're working toward has become abstract. Reconnect with your why. Reignite the motivation. Remember what this is for, and the energy that should follow from that remembering will carry you past what effort and method alone couldn't.

This response points at something real. Motivation does affect what's possible. People who care deeply about what they're doing do carry a particular energy into that work. The experience of disconnection from purpose is a genuine experience, and the reconnection with it can be a genuine shift.

The ceiling appears here with particular sharpness, because the reader who encounters it has often tried very hard to generate the motivation the approach says is missing. They have reconnected with their purpose, genuinely and repeatedly. They know why they want to move. They want to move. And they still cannot. Which means the explanation that what's missing is sufficient wanting has failed them twice: first by not producing the movement, and then by producing the silent implication that the wanting itself is inadequate.

The structural account is different. Motivation is a property of how a system is organized, not a fuel that can be supplied from outside. When the system is organized around a frame that doesn't fit the actual situation (when the gap between interpretation and reality is what's generating the stuck), motivational intensity does not close that gap. It often makes the gap more painful. The person who is highly motivated and still not moving is not experiencing a deficit of wanting. They are experiencing effort applied from a position that cannot reach where the problem lives, with a high degree of energetic engagement in that mislocated effort.

The problem is not the motivation. The problem is the position.

• • •

The fifth approach is the most sophisticated of the five, and in some ways the one that gets closest.

Acceptance. Stop fighting where you are. The pressure to change, on this account, is itself part of what's generating the suffering. You are caught in a loop of wanting to be somewhere you are not, judging yourself for not being there, and that judgment is consuming energy that could otherwise move toward what you actually want. Release the judgment. Accept the present reality. Stop making being here mean something unflattering about who you are.

This approach recognizes something that the previous four largely miss: that force is counterproductive when applied to a self-organizing system, and that some of what is being experienced as stuck is actually the experience of a system under pressure to change in a way that doesn't fit its current organization. The acceptance-based approaches are pointing at real dynamics. The relief that follows from genuinely releasing the pressure to be somewhere else is a real relief. It is not imaginary and it is not nothing.

Where it stops is precise. Acceptance resolves the self-coercion. It does not, by itself, explain the structure that was generating the stuck in the first place. A person who stops fighting themselves and finds genuine peace with where they are has done something valuable. But they have not yet, necessarily, understood why the movement they want isn't available: what is organizing their perception of the situation in a way that makes that movement not reachable from this position. Without that understanding, they are in a better place, but not yet a different one. Not yet a mobile one.

The acceptance-based approaches are a precondition for what this book describes. The release of self-coercion is necessary for the kind of understanding that actually changes position. But it is not the same thing as that understanding. And the reader who has found genuine acceptance and still finds the movement they want unavailable has encountered this limit.

• • •

Five approaches. Each genuinely useful within its territory. Each with a specific ceiling.

The ceiling, in each case, is the same ceiling approached from a different direction. Every one of these approaches works from inside the frame that is generating the stuck. They address the experience of not moving from a position that takes as given the way the situation is organized. They optimize effort, thought, method, motivation, or attitude within that organization. What none of them does is ask the prior question: does this organization fit the actual situation? Is the frame, the orientational structure within which effort is being applied, the one that makes the movement in question available?

This is not a failure of the approaches. They were not designed to ask that question. They were designed to work within frames, which is what most tools for human change are designed to do. The problem is not that they are inadequate tools. The problem is that when the frame is what needs to change, tools designed to operate within it cannot reach what's needed.

The reader for whom this book is written has encountered this ceiling at least once, and probably more than once. They have tried the approaches, found what each one could do, and run into the specific limit at which it stopped. They may have concluded, from repeated encounters with this limit, that the problem is them, that they are somehow resistant to change in a way that others are not, or that their version of stuck is too entrenched, too particular, too personal to be addressed by anything general. That conclusion is understandable. It is also incorrect. What they have encountered is not a ceiling on what is possible for them. It is a structural ceiling on approaches that operate at the wrong level.

There is a different level. The following chapters address it directly.

The question they are organized around is not how to optimize effort from the current position, or how to think differently from within the existing frame, or which method might work where others haven't. It is a prior question, and a simpler one: where is this person standing, and does that position allow the movement they want?

The answer to that question, and what becomes possible once it is answered correctly, is what the rest of this book is for.

Why Effort Fails

3. What Actually Works and How This Book Delivers It

The map

You have just finished reading about what doesn't work. Five approaches, each useful in its own territory, each with a specific ceiling, a point at which it stops producing movement because the problem lives somewhere it cannot reach. If you recognized yourself in any of those approaches, you know the ceiling not as an idea but as a felt experience: the sense of having done the right things and arrived back in the same place.

This chapter tells you what does work. Not in the form of a new approach to add to the previous five. In the form of a different understanding entirely, one that changes what you can see, which changes what becomes available, which changes what you actually do. The eight chapters that follow deliver that understanding step by step. This chapter tells you what each of them does and why they are ordered the way they are.

It is a map. And maps are useful in proportion to their accuracy. This one was drawn after the territory was fully explored, which means it can describe what you are about to encounter with precision rather than promise. Everything ahead of you exists. These are the descriptions of what is actually there.

• • •

Begin with the problem, stated as plainly as possible.

When effort fails consistently, the reason is almost never the one people reach for first. It is not insufficient willpower. It is not the wrong method. It is not that you haven't yet found the right system or the right mindset or the right level of commitment. Those explanations feel plausible because they locate the problem somewhere reachable, somewhere that more effort or better technique could address.

The actual reason is structural. You are applying effort at a level that cannot reach where the problem lives.

The problem lives in what this book calls a frame: an orientational structure that organizes what you perceive as possible, necessary, or constrained, before you consciously interpret anything. A frame is not a perspective you choose. It is the condition within which perception occurs. It is prior to your deliberate thinking, which is why deliberate thinking, applied within it, tends to confirm what the frame has already organized rather than questioning whether the frame fits.

When effort fails, the frame is almost always implicated. Not the effort. Not the person making it. The position from which the effort is being applied.

This is not a metaphor. It is a precise structural account, and the eight chapters ahead deliver it completely.

• • •

One thing about how this book works needs to be said before the map.

Most books in this territory end with a framework, a practice, or a set of steps to follow. This one doesn't. That is not modesty or incompleteness. It is structural.

Prescribing action assumes that the right behavior can be defined independently of where a specific person is standing. The field this book draws on, Applied Philosophy of Human Systems, treats that assumption as unreliable in exactly the cases where reliability is most needed. What to do follows naturally from an accurate understanding of where you are. When the understanding is genuine, action becomes obvious. When it isn't, prescribed action either fails or produces movement in the wrong direction with more energy.

What this book provides is the understanding. The action is yours.

That's not a limitation. It is the structure of how this actually works. The reader who finishes this book and doesn't have a twelve-step plan is not missing anything. They have something more useful: a different view of their own situation, from a position where more of it is visible. What they do from there does not need to be directed.

• • •

Eight chapters. Here is what each one does.

Chapter 4 builds the foundation. Before anything else in this book can land correctly, a single assumption needs to be examined, one so deeply embedded in how we talk about people and change that it rarely surfaces as an assumption at all. The assumption is that human beings are something like mechanisms:

complex, perhaps, but essentially systems that can be adjusted, repaired, and directed by applying the right intervention in the right way.

That assumption is wrong in a specific and consequential way. Human beings are self-organizing systems, not mechanisms, and that distinction changes everything about what you can expect effort to do. It changes what it means when you aren't moving. It changes what the word "stuck" actually refers to. And it changes what kind of change is possible and how it actually happens. Chapter 4 makes that reframe complete. Everything else in this book stands on it.

Chapter 5 introduces the frame. Once you understand that you are a self-organizing system, the natural question is: what is it organized around? The answer is a frame: an orientational structure that you are inside before you begin consciously thinking about anything. Frames are not perspectives you adopt. They are the conditions within which perception occurs.

The chapter takes careful account of something that makes frames difficult to work with: you cannot see the frame you are inside. Not because you lack self-awareness, but because of how frames function. Their job is to organize perception efficiently, without requiring conscious examination of every possible interpretation. A frame that surfaced for your inspection every time you needed to understand something would be useless. They work precisely because they are invisible. Chapter 5 explains what this means, why it matters, and, importantly, what it is actually possible to do about it.

Chapter 6 introduces a distinction that is central to the rest of the book. Not all change is the same kind of change. There are two genuinely different kinds, and they look nearly identical from inside them, which is why effort so often gets applied in the wrong direction with such consistent and exhausting results.

The first kind of change moves within a stable frame. The coordinates that define success remain constant, and what's needed is learning, practice, improved execution, the ordinary work of getting better at something. Effort applied here reaches the problem.

The second kind of change requires the frame itself to shift. The organizing structure that has been defining the situation, the options, and the meaning of success is part of what needs to change. Effort applied within this kind of frame cannot reach the problem. It can only confirm and reinforce the frame's existing organization. Chapter 6 explains how to tell the difference, and why misreading it is the mechanism behind some of the most familiar and painful failures of effort.

Chapter 7 reframes stuck. Not gently, and not in the way motivational language reframes things. Precisely.

The particular quality of stuck this chapter is concerned with is the kind that carries shame: the experience of knowing exactly what to do, of having decided to do it clearly and sincerely, perhaps many times, and of being unable to go. The gap between knowing and doing that has started to feel like evidence of something unflattering about who you are.

That experience is not what it appears to be. What looks like paralysis, inability to commit, or failure of will is in most cases something the book calls protective choosing: a structurally coherent, entirely rational response from a system that has organized itself around something that the proposed movement would threaten. Chapter 7 makes that visible. The reader who recognizes themselves in this description will find some release.

Not because the chapter solves the problem, but because it correctly identifies what the problem actually is, which is something the shame narrative cannot do.

Chapter 8 is the pivot. It introduces the question that changes everything, and sets it against the question that most people bring to their experience of stuck.

The question most people bring is: how do I do this better? Better strategy, better execution, more refined approach, more consistent effort. It is a question about optimization: about improving performance within a given set of parameters. This is sometimes exactly the right question. When the frame fits and the effort is well-located, optimizing within it leads somewhere useful.

But there is another question. It almost never arrives automatically, and most urgency-driven environments actively discourage it because it is slower and less immediately actionable. The question is: where am I standing? Not how to improve from this position, but whether this position is the one from which the thing in question can actually be reached. Chapter 8 explains what it means to ask that question genuinely, what it produces when you do, and why the answer to it does more, in the cases where it's the right question, than any improvement in execution could.

Chapter 9 brings everything built in the previous five chapters into contact with the specific territories of daily life where it most visibly and reliably applies.

Five domains. The first is agency: your actual, daily experience of making choices, or not making them. The second is leadership: not in the sense of formal authority, but any situation in which you are trying to influence the behavior of another person. The third is time: specifically, your relationship to what has already happened and to what has not yet happened, and the way frames organize both. The fourth is identity: who you understand yourself to be, and what happens to that understanding when the frame shifts. The fifth is the systems you are embedded in: the relationships, organizations, and institutions that carry their own organization and that push back, in their own way, when yours begins to change.

Each domain is a place where the same underlying structure plays out in recognizable, daily, concrete form. Reading about it in the abstract is one thing. Seeing it in the specific territory where you live and work is another. Chapter 9 provides the second kind of recognition.

Chapter 10 covers what most books about change do not cover: what happens after a genuine shift. Most accounts of insight end at the moment of arrival. The chapter that follows tells you why that is exactly the moment when a particular kind of confusion tends to begin.

Genuine reorganization does not arrive fully formed, stable, and permanent. It arrives incomplete, surrounded by systems that have not yet reorganized with it. The patterns that were organized around the old frame do not immediately disappear. They persist, sometimes for a significant time, as the slower-moving systems, behavioral habits, relational patterns, environments shaped by and for the previous position, gradually catch up with the shift in the frame. This can look, from inside it, like the shift wasn't real, or like you lost it, or like you are the kind of person who understands things but cannot hold them.

Chapter 10 explains what this interval actually is, why it looks the way it looks, and what it requires. It is the chapter that makes everything else sustainable.

Chapter 11 extends the full account to the work of influencing other people who are stuck. This is not a separate topic. It is the same account applied to a different subject position: what it means to work with a self-organizing system rather than to be one.

The chapter is for practitioners in the broadest sense: coaches, therapists, consultants, teachers, leaders, managers, parents, anyone who regularly finds themselves trying to help another person move through something that isn't moving. The specific contexts vary enormously. The structural situation is the same in all of them. And whether or not you have understood it as such is one of the things that most determines what your work can reach. Chapter 11 provides that understanding.

• • •

Chapter 12 closes the book with something that is not a summary and not a conclusion. It is a description, specific and warm, of what life looks like on the other side of this reframe. Not in ideal form. Not all at once. But enough that the quality of engagement with your own experience has changed in the ways this book has been describing. It is offered not as a destination you are supposed to reach, but as a recognizable portrait of what becomes possible. You will know, when you arrive there, how much of it already applies.

A note on what the book does not include, so you are not looking for it.

This book does not prescribe technique. The field it draws on has deliberate reasons for this, which will become clearer as you proceed. For now, the short version: technique applied at the wrong level from the wrong position produces effort that cannot connect. Understanding applied to an accurate reading of where you actually are allows appropriate action to become visible. What appears in this book is the understanding. The technique (if any is needed, and often what becomes available is simpler than that) is yours to recognize when the frame is right.

At the back of this book is an appendix: a companion monograph that maps the full architecture of Applied Philosophy of Human Systems, the field this book draws on. It is there for readers who finish the book and want a complete architectural picture of the ideas encountered here. It is not required. The book is complete without it.

The eight chapters between here and there are ready. They know where they are going. So do you, now. That is what a map is for.

4. You're Not Broken. You're Positioned.

Human systems and what they tell us about change

There is an assumption so widely shared that it almost never surfaces as an assumption. It operates underneath most advice about change, most systems of self-improvement, most conversations about why things aren't working. It is so basic to how we talk about human beings that questioning it feels slightly absurd: like questioning whether floors should be flat.

The assumption is this: that a human being is something like a machine.

Not in any crude or insulting sense. Not the clunky industrial machine of a century ago. Something more sophisticated: a complex mechanism with inputs and outputs, parts that can malfunction and be repaired, settings that can be adjusted, software that can be upgraded. A system where applying the right intervention in the right way produces a predictable result. Where failure to produce results means something is wrong with the mechanism, and where fixing the wrong thing restores proper function.

This assumption is everywhere. It is in the language we use for people who aren't changing ("stuck," "broken," "not working"), in the metaphors we reach for when describing what needs to happen ("fix," "repair," "reset," "retool"), in the logic of most approaches to personal development (identify the malfunction, apply the correct intervention, restore function). It shapes what we expect effort to do, what we conclude when it doesn't do it, and what we end up thinking about ourselves when the mechanism stubbornly refuses to behave like a mechanism.

It is also, in a specific and consequential way, wrong.

• • •

Human beings are not mechanisms. They are self-organizing systems. That distinction is the conceptual foundation of everything this book describes, and it is worth taking a moment to understand what it actually means: not as an abstract claim about philosophy of mind, but as a practical description of something you have almost certainly already observed about yourself and the people around you.

A mechanism is assembled from outside. Its parts are put together according to a design, and they interact according to rules defined by that design. Change a mechanism, and you change it: the alteration holds, the new configuration is stable, the result is predictable. Apply the right force at the right point and you get the right outcome. Mechanisms do what they are made to do.

A self-organizing system is different in kind. It generates its own structure through ongoing interaction with its environment. It is not assembled; it emerges. It is not directed by a central controller; it maintains itself through continuous, distributed adjustment happening simultaneously at many levels. And it responds to outside pressure not by simply receiving and transmitting that pressure, but by interpreting it, integrating it, sometimes absorbing it, sometimes resisting it, always through the lens of its own existing organization.

Clouds are self-organizing systems. Markets are self-organizing systems. Ecosystems are self-organizing systems. And so, most relevantly, are human beings.

Your thoughts, emotions, behaviors, habits, identities, and meanings are not independent components that someone could rearrange by reaching in and moving them around. They are expressions of an ongoing process of self-organization, emerging continuously from the interaction between you and your environment, shaped by your history, your relationships, your physical state, and the meanings you carry from every experience that has mattered. They are organized. And they reorganize through the same process that organized them in the first place: through accumulated experience, through contact with what is real, through conditions that gradually or suddenly make a different organization available.

This is not a mystical claim. It is a description of how you actually work, at the level that matters for understanding why effort sometimes produces movement and sometimes doesn't.

● ● ●

Here is what this means in practice.

Change is not something done to you. It is something that unfolds within you when conditions shift. This is not a passive description. Conditions can be influenced, and the chapters ahead will have a great deal to say about how. But it reframes what you can expect effort to do, and more importantly, what you can conclude when effort doesn't do it.

When a mechanism doesn't function correctly, the problem is in the mechanism. But when a self-organizing system doesn't move in a particular direction, the problem is almost never in the system's capacity. It is in the conditions. Specifically, it is in whether the conditions make the movement available.

A person who isn't changing isn't broken. They are organized in a way that doesn't currently produce the change in question. That organization is responsive to conditions, meaning it can shift when conditions shift. It is not a fixed defect. It is a current state that reflects what the system has been navigating.

The difference between these two descriptions, broken mechanism versus organized system responding to conditions, is not merely semantic. It completely changes what you look at when things aren't working. With the mechanism model, you look for the malfunction: what is wrong with this person, what part of them is broken, what needs to be fixed. With the self-organizing system model, you look at position: where is this person standing, what is the system organized around, and does that position allow the movement in question?

Position is something that can change. And it changes very differently than a broken mechanism gets repaired.

• • •

There is something that follows from this that is worth naming directly, because it runs against almost everything the usual approaches assume.

Force doesn't work on self-organizing systems the way it works on mechanisms.

Apply force to a mechanism and you move it: the lever pushes, the gear turns, the output changes. Apply force to a self-organizing system and something quite different happens. The system interprets the force. It assesses whether the pressure can be integrated into its existing organization: absorbed, adapted to, made part of how it moves. If it can, the system reorganizes to incorporate it. If it can't, the system resists.

That resistance is not defiance. It is not obstinacy or fear or weakness. It is the system doing exactly what it is designed to do: protecting its own coherence against pressure that would require it to contradict its own organization. The resistance is self-preservation. It is the system functioning correctly.

This is why force (whether applied from outside by someone trying to help, or from inside by a person trying to make themselves change) so rarely produces lasting results. At the surface, the system may comply. The person says the right things, takes the required steps, adopts the new behavior. But at the level where the system's actual organization is maintained, nothing has shifted. The moment the force is removed (the moment the accountability structure relaxes, the coaching session ends, the initial motivation fades), the system reasserts the patterns that were there before. Not because the person didn't try. Because the system was never actually reorganized. It was temporarily overridden.

You have almost certainly experienced this. The resolution that held for three weeks and then quietly dissolved. The insight from the workshop that felt transformative on Friday and was somehow gone by Wednesday. The commitment you made and meant and then watched yourself not keep, not from lack of caring but from something that felt like a deeper and more stubborn layer asserting itself underneath the commitment. That layer is the system's organization. It is not your enemy. It is you, at a level that force cannot reach.

• • •

Now consider what we habitually do with this experience.

We conclude that we didn't try hard enough. That our commitment wasn't genuine. That something is wrong with us at the level of character or will or desire. We intensify the force and apply it inward: more discipline, more self-criticism, more pressure to be different than we are. We add the weight of self-judgment to the structural pressure that was already there.

What this produces, reliably, is not change. It is exhaustion. The energy cost of maintaining force against the system's own resistance is enormous. And it compounds the problem by treating the resistance itself (which is structural and appropriate) as evidence of personal failure. The person who is most hard on themselves for not changing is often the person applying the most force to the most resistant system, and interpreting each resistance as confirmation that they are the problem.

They are not the problem. They are standing somewhere from which the change they want is not currently available. That is a different situation entirely. And it requires a different response.

• • •

This is what the self-organizing system model actually offers: not a new set of techniques for producing change, but a more accurate description of what you are working with when you are trying to produce it.

You are working with a system that organizes through meaning rather than through force. A system that responds to interpretation, not just pressure. A system that resists what it cannot integrate and absorbs what it can. A system that maintains itself through distributed processes mostly operating below the threshold of conscious control, which means that conscious effort reaches some things and not others, and the parts it doesn't reach are not thereby inaccessible, just inaccessible through that particular lever.

You are also working with a system that is not fixed. The organization you are currently in is a current state, not a permanent condition. It reflects the position you're standing in, the frame that is currently organizing your perception of what is possible, the conditions that are currently either making movement available or making it unavailable. All of those can change. They change in response to conditions, which is why understanding conditions matters more than intensifying effort.

The shift from the mechanism model to the self-organizing system model changes the primary question you ask when things aren't working. The mechanism question is: what is wrong with me, and how do I fix it? The self-organizing system question is: where am I standing, and does that position allow what I'm trying to do?

The first question points toward self-correction, self-discipline, and the application of more of what hasn't been working. The second points toward something prior: understanding the structure of the situation, which is different from understanding what's wrong with the person in the situation. Position can be worked with. Character verdicts mostly can't.

• • •

You are not broken.

That is not a reassurance. It is a structural claim. Broken is a mechanical description that does not apply to self-organizing systems. A self-organizing system that isn't producing a particular kind of movement is not malfunctioning. It is organized in a way that does not currently make that movement available. Those are genuinely different situations. The first calls for repair. The second calls for understanding.

You are positioned. You are standing somewhere, in a particular orientation toward your circumstances, organized around a particular way of understanding what is happening and what is possible. That position has a history: it reflects what you have navigated, what you have concluded, what has been required of you. It is not arbitrary, and it is not a failure. It is where the system has organized itself in response to real conditions.

And position can change. Not through force. Not through intensified self-criticism or redoubled discipline or the discovery of the right technique. Through understanding: a clearer view of where you are standing, what is organizing your perception of the situation, and what would actually need to shift for the movement you want to become available.

That understanding is what this book is offering. Not a plan for where to go. That follows naturally once you can see clearly where you are. A way of looking that replaces the question "what is wrong with me?" with the question that can actually be answered: "where am I standing, and what does this position tell me about what needs to shift?"

Chapter 5 takes the next step: the specific structure that organizes that position. The thing that is so close to you that you almost certainly have never seen it directly. The thing that determines, before you consciously interpret anything, what seems possible, what seems necessary, and what seems out of reach.

It has a name. And naming it changes what you can do about it.

5. The Structure You're Already Inside

What frames are and why you can't see yours

There is a word that gets used so casually in conversations about personal growth that it has nearly lost its meaning. Reframe. Reframe how you see the situation. Reframe the problem as an opportunity. Reframe failure as feedback. The instruction is offered as though seeing differently were simply a matter of deciding to, the way you might decide to look left instead of right. As though perception were a camera you could point wherever you chose.

This book uses a different word, and it means something importantly different. Not a reframe: a frame.

A frame is not a perspective you adopt. It is not a way of looking that you consciously select from a menu of available ways of looking. It is the structure that organizes what you perceive as possible, necessary, or constrained before you consciously look at anything. It is prior to interpretation. It is the condition within which interpretation occurs.

If that sounds abstract, consider this: you have almost certainly walked into a room full of people and known, within seconds and without any deliberate analysis, whether you were among friends or among strangers, whether the energy was welcoming or tense, whether you were in a situation you understood or one that required caution. That assessment did not follow from conscious reasoning. It preceded it. Something organized your perception of the room before you thought about the room. That something is the frame.

Or consider the experience of reading an email from a colleague and feeling, immediately and before you've finished the first sentence, that something is off, that there is a subtext, a tension, something being communicated beneath the words. You may not be able to say what it is. But the frame has already organized the message as one kind of thing rather than another. By the time you reach the conclusion and start forming a conscious interpretation, the frame has already done most of the work.

Frames are not unusual. They are not the province of people with issues. They are the operating condition of every human being in every waking moment. The question is never whether you have one. It is whether the one you have fits the situation you are in.

• • •

Here is the thing that matters most about frames, and the thing that is hardest to fully absorb: you cannot see the frame you are inside.

Not because it is hidden from you. Not because you lack sufficient self-awareness or intelligence or willingness to look. But because of how frames function. Their job is to organize perception efficiently, without requiring conscious processing of every possible interpretation of every situation you encounter. A frame that surfaced for your inspection every time you needed to understand something would be useless. You would spend your entire life examining the lens instead of seeing through it. Frames work precisely because they are transparent. You look through them, not at them. What you see through a frame looks like reality, not like one organization of reality among other possible organizations.

This is not a metaphor. It is a description of how the thing actually operates.

Think about color. A person who has worn tinted lenses long enough stops seeing the tint. The world simply looks that color. The correction feels like clarity rather than distortion. Now imagine that the tint is not on a lens you can remove but in the perceptual system itself, organized through years of experience, reinforced through emotional association, maintained through habitual response. That is closer to what a frame is. And that is why the instruction to "look at things differently" misses what it is trying to address. You cannot simply choose to look differently when the structure doing the looking is the thing that would need to change.

This also explains something that most people have experienced but found difficult to account for. You recognize, intellectually, that a particular way of seeing a situation is not serving you. You can explain, articulately and in detail, why the interpretation is limited. And then you continue feeling and responding as though the limited interpretation were true. Not because you are being irrational. Because the frame is maintained at a level below where rational argument operates. Knowing the frame is there does not dissolve it. The frame continues organizing perception regardless of what you have concluded about it.

• • •

Frames are not maintained through conscious thought. They are maintained through emotional weighting, through habitual response, through meaning structures that have been reinforced so consistently and for so long that they operate automatically. This is why the same situation can produce completely different responses in the same person at different times, not because the situation changed, but because something in the frame shifted, and the shift wasn't chosen.

It is also why the same situation produces completely different responses in different people. Two people attend the same difficult conversation and leave with fundamentally different accounts of what happened, not because one of them is lying or wrong, but because the frames through which they organized the conversation were genuinely different. Each person's account is accurate to their frame. The disagreement is not about facts. It is between organizational structures that determined which facts were salient, which were ignored, and what the salient facts meant.

This is disorienting to really take in, because it undermines the intuition that if you just think clearly enough, look carefully enough, and stay open enough, you will eventually arrive at the correct perception of the situation. That intuition assumes a view from nowhere, a perceptual position outside the frame from which the frame can be assessed against unmediated reality. That position does not exist. Every perception is organized by a frame. The question is not whether to have one but whether the one you have fits what is actually happening.

What does fit mean? A frame fits when the organization it imposes on experience is accurate enough to the actual conditions that movement through those conditions becomes possible.

When interpretation aligns closely enough with what is real that effort connects with what effort can actually change. When what seems possible and what is actually possible roughly correspond. The person operating from a fitting frame can act, can course-correct when feedback arrives, can distinguish between situations that require more of what they're already doing and situations that require something different.

A frame that doesn't fit does something quite specific. It makes effort feel like pushing against something that shouldn't be as hard as it is. It produces the experience of working and not arriving. It generates consistent feedback that something is wrong without generating clarity about what. And because the frame is transparent, because the person inside it is looking through it, not at it, the most natural conclusion is not that the frame is the problem but that the effort is insufficient, the method is wrong, the person is lacking something.

That conclusion is what Chapter 4 was about. The frame is not a personal failure. It is a structural condition.

· · ·

There is a specific implication that follows from all of this, and it is the reason this chapter sits where it does in the book.

Most effort (the effort to change, improve, get unstuck, build something new, become someone different) is applied from within the frame rather than to it.

This is almost inevitable, because the frame is what you are inside when you decide to make an effort. It organizes what the problem is, what the solutions look like, what success would mean, what resources are available. The frame defines the space within which your effort makes sense and the space within which the approaches you try seem like reasonable approaches.

And then the effort is made inside that space, thoughtfully, sincerely, often with great discipline, and arrives at the ceiling of what that space allows.

This is not a failure of the effort. It is a structural limitation of where the effort is being directed. You can optimize extensively within a frame. You can become highly skilled at working within a particular organization of reality. You can refine, improve, get better and better at the thing the frame defines as the thing to get better at. And if the frame doesn't fit the actual situation, all of that refinement produces increasingly sophisticated movement in a direction that doesn't serve.

The person who has tried every available approach to a problem that won't move is often in exactly this situation. Not because the approaches were poor. Because each of them, however different they appeared on the surface, was being tried from within the same frame that was organizing the problem in the first place. The approaches changed. The organizational structure within which the approaches were evaluated remained constant. And at that level, nothing shifted.

• • •

Now comes the part that is most important and most difficult to sit with.

Frame shifts cannot be produced by deciding to have one.

This sounds like a counsel of helplessness. It is not. But it does require setting aside an assumption that runs very deep in most thinking about personal change, the assumption that if you understand what needs to be different, and you commit sincerely to making it different, and you apply that commitment with sufficient discipline, the change will follow.

At the level of behavior, this is sometimes true. At the level of frames, it almost never is.

A frame shift is a reorganization of the structure through which perception itself is organized. It happens at a level below where deliberate commitment operates. Conscious intention can participate in the conditions that make a shift possible. It cannot produce the shift through force of will, because the frame is not maintained by will. It is maintained through emotional weighting, habitual response, and meaning structures that operate largely outside conscious control. Applying conscious intention against the frame tends to reinforce it, because the effort takes the frame as the stable ground from which it is being made.

What does produce frame shifts? Three things appear consistently.

The first is lived contradiction, the accumulated experience of the frame failing to fit reality often enough and clearly enough that its organization becomes unstable. This is not intellectual recognition that the frame is limited. It is the visceral, repeated experience of acting from the frame and arriving somewhere wrong. The prediction the frame generates doesn't match what actually happens. The response the frame organizes produces results the frame didn't anticipate. Over time, if the contradictions accumulate without being explained away, the frame's stability erodes.

The second is exposure to an alternative organization that fits better, not as an argument, but as a living example or a genuinely inhabitable perspective. When someone who has been inside a particular frame encounters another person or context organized differently, and the different organization is coherent and visible, something becomes available that wasn't before. Not a decision to adopt the alternative, but an orientation toward it that makes a shift possible.

The third is simply time and conditions that reduce the pressure maintaining the existing frame, situations in which the frame doesn't need to be defended, in which an alternative organization can be occupied without threat, in which the person is not required to act from the existing frame and can, for a time, stand somewhere different.

None of these is a technique. None of them can be scheduled. What they suggest is that the appropriate response to a frame problem is not effort but attention, attention to where contradictions are appearing, to what alternative organizations are available, to what conditions would allow the existing frame's stability to ease. That is a different kind of engagement than most approaches to change ask for.

• • •

Before moving on, it is worth noting what "reframing" (the instruction to look at things differently) actually is when it works.

It is not the conscious adoption of a new perspective through decision. It is sometimes a pointer toward an existing instability in the frame, a way of gesturing at a place where the current organization is already showing strain, where the lived contradiction has already done some of its work, where the alternative is already dimly available. When reframing works, it is because the frame was already ready to shift and the reframe names the direction. When it doesn't work (when the new perspective slides off, when the person nods and returns to the old organization within hours), it is because the frame was not ready. The instability wasn't there. The gesture landed on stable ground rather than on the crack that was opening.

This is not a criticism of reframing as a practice. It is a description of its actual mechanism. Understanding the mechanism tells you when to use it and why it sometimes works and sometimes doesn't, which is more useful than either believing in it universally or dismissing it.

Understanding frames in general tells you something more important: when the problem you are working on is located at the frame level, the tools appropriate to work at other levels will not reach it. And the first step toward reaching it is seeing it, recognizing that the structure you are inside is a structure, not reality itself. That recognition, even partial and preliminary, is the beginning of what the next chapters describe.

Chapter 6 takes the structure one step further. It explains a specific and consequential error that follows almost automatically from being inside a frame that doesn't fit, an error so common it accounts for more exhausted, stuck, trying-everything-and-arriving-nowhere experience than almost any other single factor.

The error has to do with effort. Not too little of it. The wrong kind.

6. Why Harder Doesn't Help

Two kinds of change and the mistake that exhausts everything

Imagine two people. Both are stuck. Both are sincere. Both have tried, with genuine effort and genuine commitment, to change something that matters to them. Neither has arrived anywhere close to where they intended.

The first person is learning a language. She has studied for six months, attended classes, used the apps, listened to podcasts during her commute. Her vocabulary has grown. Her pronunciation has improved. She can construct sentences she couldn't have managed in January. But she still can't hold a conversation without stalling, still loses the thread when native speakers talk at natural speed, still translates internally before she speaks. She is frustrated by her pace, but the frustration is the ordinary frustration of a long project: she is moving, just not as fast as she wants.

The second person is trying to leave a marriage he has known for three years is ending. He has read books about it. He has talked to a therapist. He has made the decision, clearly and deliberately, at least a dozen times. He knows what he thinks, knows what he values, knows that staying is damaging both of them. And he cannot move. Not from fear of the practical consequences (he has thought through those carefully). From something he cannot name. Something that holds him in the same place every time he gets close to actually doing the thing he has decided to do.

These two people are not having the same problem. They are having problems that look similar from the outside (both involve effort that hasn't yet produced the desired result) but are different in kind. And the difference matters enormously, because the response that helps one of them will not help the other. May, in fact, make things actively worse.

• • •

The first kind of change moves within a stable frame.

The coordinates within which progress is defined remain constant. Learning a language is translational change: the goal is clear, the direction is sound, the frame is intact, and the work is refinement within it: more vocabulary, more exposure, more practice until the neural pathways consolidate and the language stops feeling foreign. What this kind of change requires is exactly what it looks like it requires: sustained effort, good method, patience with the pace of incremental progress. It responds to discipline. It accumulates. Given enough of it, applied in the right direction, it arrives.

Most of what we think of as personal development is translational change. Building a skill. Establishing a habit. Improving a relationship through better communication. Growing a business through better execution. Developing a practice. All of these operate within a stable frame: a coherent understanding of what is being done and why, within which progress can be measured and effort can be well-directed. Translational change is real, it is valuable, and it is what most systems of personal development, coaching, and performance optimization are designed to produce.

There is nothing wrong with translational change. The problem arises only when it is applied to a situation that requires something different.

• • •

The second kind of change reorganizes the frame itself.

It is not movement within stable coordinates. It is a shift in the coordinates: a reorganization of the structure through which the situation is being understood, through which the options are being perceived, through which the meaning of action and inaction are being organized. After this kind of change, what was previously invisible becomes apparent. What seemed necessary reveals itself as optional. What appeared impossible opens up. The situation hasn't changed. The structure through which it is being organized has. And that structural change alters everything that follows from it.

The man who cannot leave his marriage is not in a translational situation. He does not need more information, better technique, or firmer commitment. He is in a frame (a deeply organized way of understanding himself, his life, his obligations, his identity, what leaving would mean and what it would make him) that does not yet have a sustainable path forward available within it. The decision he keeps making is real. It is also being made from within a structure that cannot yet support it. And so the decision is made and the movement doesn't follow, made again and doesn't follow again, each time reinforcing the conclusion that something is wrong with him rather than recognizing that the problem is structural.

Transformational change cannot be scheduled or produced by intensified effort. It occurs when the existing frame becomes sufficiently unstable, when accumulated experience, lived contradiction, or exposure to genuine alternatives creates enough instability in the current organization that a different structure becomes available. This is a process that happens largely at the level described in Chapter 5: below the threshold of conscious control, through conditions rather than through decisions. The man does not need to decide harder. He needs something to shift at the level where the decision is being blocked.

That something is not something he can force. But it is something that can be supported, and understanding what kind of change the situation requires is the first move toward supporting it rather than fighting it.

• • •

Here is the failure mode, stated as plainly as possible.

When effort isn't working, the most natural response is to apply more of it. This is not irrational. In translational situations, more effort (better directed, more consistent, more disciplined) is often exactly what is needed. The logic is sound for the situations it fits.

But when applied to a transformational situation, more translational effort does not just fail to help. It makes things worse.

Here is why. The frame is the structure the effort is being made from. When you redouble your effort within a frame that isn't shifting, you are investing more deeply in that frame's organization. You are taking it more seriously as the ground from which the work is being done. You are reinforcing its stability at the precise moment when what is needed is for that stability to ease. The effort is anchoring the structure it is trying to change, because the effort is being made from within the structure rather than toward it.

This is the mechanism behind one of the most common and most demoralizing experiences in the territory of personal change: the person who has tried harder and found that things became more stuck, not less. Who has increased their discipline and found that the gap between effort and result has widened rather than closed. Who has committed more fully and found that the commitment itself has become a source of pain, because it keeps arriving at the same wall.

That person is not failing. That person is applying a translational solution to a transformational problem. The effort is real. The commitment is genuine. The direction is wrong: not pointing the wrong way, but operating at the wrong level entirely.

• • •

There is a quality to this experience that is worth describing precisely, because it is distinctive enough to be recognizable once named.

Translational effort that hasn't worked yet feels like being behind. There is a sense of distance between where you are and where you intend to be, a clear direction to close that distance, and the feeling that more of what you're already doing (more consistently applied, over more time) will eventually arrive. The effort is tiring in the way that long work is tiring: real cost, real accumulation, a reasonable expectation of eventual result.

Translational effort applied to a transformational situation feels like pushing against something that shouldn't be there. There is effort going out that isn't connecting with anything. Progress that resets. Ground gained that doesn't hold. A sense not of distance from the goal but of something at the goal itself that won't yield, something structural and resistant that more effort seems to make more solid rather than less. And accompanying all of this, the slow accumulation of a particular conclusion: that the resistance must be coming from inside, from some inadequacy in the person applying the effort.

That conclusion is wrong in a specific and important way. The resistance is coming from the frame. It is not a character assessment. It is structural information: a signal that the effort is hitting the ceiling of what translational engagement can reach. The appropriate response to that signal is not more effort. It is a different level of engagement.

• • •

A question follows naturally here, and it is worth taking seriously: how do you know which kind of change a situation requires?

There is no formula, but there are signals.

Translational change is appropriate when consistent effort is producing movement that corresponds roughly to the effort applied, when more practice produces more skill, when more attention produces more progress, when the direction feels right even when the work is hard. The experience is of distance being closed. The feedback is meaningful. The map corresponds to the territory. Even when the pace is frustrating, there is a quality of forward movement that is absent in the alternative.

Transformational change is required when consistent effort produces either no movement or movement that doesn't satisfy in the way movement should satisfy. When doing more of what's working starts to feel like doing more of what isn't. When the goal, achieved or approached, feels different from how it was supposed to feel, hollow in a way that is hard to account for, or blocked in a way that doesn't respond to better execution. When the question that keeps surfacing is not "how do I do this better" but something prior: whether the thing is right, whether this is the right direction at all, whether the frame within which the goal was defined still fits the person you are now.

Another signal: the frame. When the same effort that has worked in other areas of your life fails consistently in one particular area (when you can point to real capability that seems unavailable here), the problem is often localized to how that specific area is being organized. The capability exists. The frame through which this domain is being understood is not allowing it to connect with what the situation actually requires.

None of these signals is conclusive on its own. But taken together (the effort that doesn't connect, the progress that doesn't hold, the satisfaction that doesn't arrive, the capability that is present elsewhere but unavailable here), they point in a direction worth attending to.

• • •

Return to the two people from the beginning of this chapter.

The language learner does not need a new kind of engagement. She needs more time and more practice and more exposure, and eventually the language will settle into something fluent. The frustration is real, but it is translational frustration: the gap between where she is and where she intends to be, closeable through continued effort in the direction she is already going. She is not stuck in the sense this book is concerned with. She is in the middle of a long project that is proceeding correctly.

The man who cannot leave his marriage needs something different, and it is not what he has been applying. More deliberation will not help. More commitment to the decision will not help. More therapy, if the therapy continues to help him understand what he already understands, will not help. What might help is engagement at the level where the blockage actually lives, not at the level of the decision, but at the level of the frame within which the decision is being made. The organizational structure that is making sustainable movement unavailable. That structure is what needs to shift. And it will shift not through force but through the conditions that allow frame reorganization to occur.

Understanding this distinction does not immediately change anything external. The man is still where he is. But it changes what he looks at. Instead of asking what is wrong with his commitment, he can ask what is organizing the situation at a level below commitment. Instead of applying more pressure to the thing that won't move, he can attend to the structure that is holding it. That shift in attention is not passive. It is a reorientation toward the level where the actual work is.

Chapter 7 goes further into what that level looks like from the inside: specifically, what is actually happening when you cannot move, and why the experience of paralysis, of being unable to commit or sustain movement you've attempted, is not what it appears to be from within the frame that is generating it.

7. What Stuck Actually Is

Agency, protective choosing, and what your paralysis is telling you

There is a particular quality of stuck that is different from all the others, and most people who have experienced it carry a specific shame about it that they do not carry about simpler versions of not moving.

It is not the stuck of not knowing what to do. It is not the stuck of facing a genuinely hard problem without a clear solution. Those kinds of stuck are uncomfortable, but they do not produce shame, because they are obviously explained by external conditions. The problem is hard. Of course you're not through it yet.

The stuck that carries shame is the one where you know exactly what to do. Where the path forward is clear. Where you have decided, perhaps many times, and meant it each time. Where you can articulate what is needed with precision and detail, can describe what success would look like, can explain the costs of not moving, and still cannot get yourself to go. Where each morning begins with a fresh resolve and each evening finds you in the same place. Where the gap between what you know and what you do has become its own source of suffering, because it seems to confirm something unflattering about who you are.

This kind of stuck is not what it appears to be. And the shame it carries is based on a misidentification of what is actually happening. This chapter makes that misidentification visible, precisely enough, it is hoped, that the reader who recognizes themselves in this description feels something shift, or ease.

• • •

Begin with agency, because the way we understand agency is the source of most of the confusion.

The prevailing model of agency treats it as a fixed capacity: something a person has more or less of, something that can be cultivated through discipline and eroded through indulgence, something that functions like a muscle: stronger in some people, weaker in others, but essentially a property of the individual that remains relatively stable across contexts. In this model, a person who isn't moving lacks agency. They have insufficient willpower. They need to strengthen the muscle, develop better habits, commit more fully, want it more.

This model generates a specific and predictable response when someone finds themselves unable to move despite genuine desire to: try harder. Add more accountability. Raise the stakes. Increase the pressure. Apply more of the only tool the model offers, which is force directed inward. And when that doesn't work, conclude that the problem is with the person. Not enough will. Not enough want. Not enough character.

The model is wrong in a specific and consequential way. Not wrong about everything (agency is real, and it does vary between people and across contexts, and some of that variation reflects genuine differences in capacity and development). But it is wrong about what agency fundamentally is, and that error in understanding is the source of most of the misapplied effort and misplaced shame in this territory.

Agency is not a fixed property. It is an emergent one. It arises, or fails to arise, from the relationship between how a situation is being organized and what that organization makes available. It expands when interpretation aligns with actual conditions: when the frame fits, when the position is sound, when the system has access to paths it can actually move along. It contracts when interpretation is misaligned: when the frame doesn't fit, when the system is standing somewhere from which the movement it needs is not currently available.

A person with contracted agency is not a person who lacks strength. They are a person whose current position does not make movement available. That is a structural description. It points to something that can change, not through increased effort (which applies force to a system that is already resisting force) but through a shift in position, which changes what the system has access to.

• • •

This reframe of agency opens onto something harder to name, because it describes an experience that is both very common and very poorly understood.

A self-organizing system, when it is functioning well, does not commit to things it cannot sustain. It assesses, continuously and largely below conscious awareness, whether available options are genuinely viable: whether they can be chosen, held, and acted on without the system working against itself to maintain them. When an option appears available but the system's assessment is that committing to it would produce more damage than the discomfort of remaining uncommitted, the system does something that looks, from the outside, like failure of will.

It chooses not to commit.

This is not a failure of will. It is the system functioning correctly. The assessment is accurate: the options currently visible are not options the system can sustain. And so it protects itself from committing to something that would cost more than the protection is worth. This is what might be called protective choosing, and it is the source of a great deal of the paralysis that gets attributed to fear, avoidance, laziness, or insufficient motivation.

The word that matters most in that description is accurate. The system is not misreading the situation. It is not being irrational or overcautious. It is making an accurate assessment that the visible options, as they currently stand, do not offer a sustainable path. The protection is not disproportionate. It is the right response to the actual structural condition.

This means that the experience of not being able to commit (of deciding and then not doing, of resolving and then finding the resolution hollow by the following week, of wanting to move and finding oneself still in the same place) is not evidence of a character flaw. It is the system accurately reporting a condition. The condition is: there is no path forward here that I can actually hold. Not yet.

· · ·

Here is where this gets subtle, because protective choosing and avoidance can look identical from the outside, and sometimes from the inside as well.

Avoidance is the system declining to engage with something it could engage with, pulling back from difficulty that is uncomfortable but navigable, staying away from a situation that is challenging but accessible. Avoidance is genuinely counterproductive: it reinforces the frame that makes the situation seem more threatening than it is, it deprives the system of the feedback that would allow the frame to adjust, it makes the avoided thing larger over time rather than smaller.

Protective choosing is different. It is the system declining to commit to something it genuinely cannot sustain, not because it is uncomfortable, but because committing would require the system to organize itself around something that contradicts its current coherence. It is the marriage that truly cannot be entered yet, not avoided out of cold feet but genuinely not available because the internal conditions that would make the commitment sustainable are not in place. It is the career change that is known to be right but cannot be made because the frame that would support the change has not yet stabilized enough to build on. It is the apology that is meant but cannot be fully made because something in the relationship is still being processed at a level below where the apology lives.

The distinction between these two (protective choosing and avoidance) cannot be made by formula. It requires honest attention to the specific situation. But there is a quality to protective choosing that, once recognized, is relatively distinguishable. Protective choosing has weight. It does not feel like relief: the relief that avoidance produces, however temporary. It feels like holding a tension that hasn't resolved, like standing at a threshold that is not yet crossable, like waiting for something that has not yet arrived. There is often something in the person that wants to move and cannot find the ground to move from. That specific combination (genuine desire, genuine inability, no relief in the not-moving) is a useful signal.

Avoidance, by contrast, tends to produce a reduction in tension at the moment of pulling back, followed by an increase over time as the avoided thing continues to grow. The relief is real in the short term. That relief is part of what makes avoidance self-reinforcing. Protective choosing does not offer that reduction. The tension remains because the situation remains genuinely unresolved.

• • •

If protective choosing is the accurate response to a structural condition, then forcing commitment is the specific thing most likely to make that condition worse.

This is the counterintuitive core of this chapter. The intervention that looks most obvious from the outside (more accountability, higher stakes, firmer commitment, increased pressure to decide) is precisely the intervention most likely to produce decisions that collapse. Not because the person is weak, but because the force is being applied to override the mechanism that is accurately protecting the system from committing to something it cannot sustain.

When someone commits under that pressure, what actually happens? The system selects an option. The selection is real. But the conditions that would make the selection sustainable have not changed: the frame is still the same, the internal organization is still the same, the structural reasons the commitment wasn't available are still present. The person has chosen. And then the choice has to be maintained through continuous effort against the system's own organization, because the system is not organized around the choice. It was not ready for the choice. The choice was made over its accurate assessment.

This is why forced commitments so often collapse at exactly the moment when the external pressure relaxes. The accountability structure that produced the commitment is removed, and the system reasserts the organization that was there before. The person experiences this as failure, as proof that their commitment wasn't genuine, as further evidence of the character problem they suspected they had. It is not any of those things. It is a self-organizing system reverting to its actual organization once the force that was overriding it is removed.

The appropriate response to protective choosing is not more pressure. It is attention to the conditions that would allow resourceful options to become available.

• • •

Which brings us to what actually changes.

A resourceful option is an alternative the system can actually sustain without continuous effort to maintain it. Not a comfortable option, necessarily (some of the most important choices a person makes are difficult, costly, and genuinely hard). But difficult in the way that good hard things are difficult: the commitment fits the system's actual organization, the direction aligns with what actually matters, the cost is real and bearable rather than real and self-contradicting. The choice can be held because the system is organized to hold it, not because external pressure is making it impossible to put down.

Resourceful options become available when certain conditions shift. When the frame that has been organizing the situation begins to change, not through force but through the processes described in the previous two chapters. When the internal contradictions that were preventing a sustainable path from emerging begin to resolve. When orientation becomes clearer, when what actually matters clarifies, when the pressure to commit before the system is ready reduces sufficiently that the system can assess its actual situation rather than responding to urgency.

There is an experience that accompanies the arrival of a resourceful option that is worth describing, because it is distinctive and recognizable. It is the experience of a decision becoming obvious. Not easy, necessarily. Not without cost. But obvious: the choice that was impossible for months or years simply becomes available, clearly, without drama. The person looks at the situation and finds that they know what to do, not because they suddenly decided more firmly, not because they received new information that resolved the question, but because something in the underlying organization has shifted and the path is now visible in a way it was not before.

This experience is sometimes misread as a change in the external situation, or as finally finding the right advice, or as some combination of factors that "landed" differently than before. It is often none of those things. It is the system reporting that it has reorganized sufficiently that a sustainable path is now accessible. The decision follows from the reorganization. It was not the cause of it.

• • •

Return to the person described at the beginning of this chapter.

The one who knows exactly what to do and cannot do it. Who has decided and not moved, resolved and not held the resolution, committed and watched the commitment dissolve within days or weeks. Who carries shame about this that sits heavier than the stuckness itself, because it seems to confirm something fundamental and unflattering.

Here is what is actually happening. The system is standing somewhere from which a sustainable path forward is not yet available. It is accurately reporting that condition through what looks, from the inside and outside, like paralysis. It is protecting itself from commitments it cannot hold, not from cowardice, not from insufficient desire, not from a defect in character, but from an accurate reading of its own current organization. The shame is not evidence of the problem. It is an addition to the problem: a layer of self-judgment applied on top of a structural condition, which adds weight without adding information.

What the situation requires is not more pressure to commit. It is attention to the conditions that are maintaining the frame that is organizing the situation in a way that makes sustainable movement unavailable. That attention is a different kind of work than the effort to commit harder. It is slower, less visible, less amenable to accountability structures and external milestones. But it is the work that reaches the level where the actual problem lives.

Stuck is not a verdict. It is structural information. It says: the movement you're attempting is not currently available from where you're standing. That is not a statement about you. It is a statement about position. And position can change.

Chapter 8 takes up the question of what that attention actually looks like: specifically, the shift from asking how do I do this better to asking where am I standing. That shift is simpler than it sounds. And it changes more than any technique that stays inside the frame where the question was already being asked.

8. The Question That Changes Everything

Orientation, optimization, and what to ask instead

There is a question that most people bring to their experience of stuck, effortful, and not-working. It is so natural that it barely registers as a choice. It is simply the question that arrives, automatically, when things are not going as intended.

The question is: how do I do this better?

Better strategy. Better execution. Better consistency. Better method. More refined, more disciplined, more carefully considered approach to the thing that isn't moving. The question assumes that the direction is sound and the frame is intact, and that what is needed is improvement within them. It is a question about optimization: about refining performance within a given set of parameters.

This is sometimes exactly the right question. When the frame fits, when the direction is sound, when effort is well-located and the problem is simply one of execution or consistency, how do I do this better leads somewhere useful. The answer to it is genuinely the answer to the problem.

But there is another question, one that almost never arrives automatically, one that most urgency-driven environments actively discourage because it is slower and less immediately actionable. It is the question this chapter is about. And it changes more, when it is actually the right question to ask, than any improvement in execution could.

The question is: where am I standing?

• • •

These two questions look superficially similar. Both are about improving a situation. Both take the person's experience of difficulty as their starting point. Both are, in their own contexts, genuinely productive.

But they operate at completely different levels, and that difference in level is everything.

How do I do this better assumes that the frame organizing the situation is accurate, and asks how to move more effectively within it. It takes the definition of the problem as given, the range of available options as given, the measure of success as given. All of those are defined by the frame. The question then seeks to optimize performance against those definitions.

Where am I standing asks something prior. It asks about the frame itself: about the structure that is organizing what seems possible, necessary, and constrained before any assessment of how to perform better begins. It does not assume that the definition of the problem is accurate, or that the options visible within the current frame are the only available options, or that the measure of success embedded in the current organization still serves. It is a question about position before it is a question about performance.

The difference is not subtle in its consequences. A person who asks how do I do this better when the actual problem is that they are standing somewhere from which the movement they want is not available will produce increasingly refined versions of stuck. They will become more skilled at working within a frame that doesn't fit. They will improve their performance in a direction that doesn't serve. And because improvement in that direction is visible and measurable, it will be genuinely difficult to recognize that the fundamental problem has not been addressed.

• • •

Optimization is not the enemy. This is worth saying clearly, because what follows can sound like a dismissal of competence, discipline, and the genuine value of getting better at things. It is not.

Optimization (refining performance within a given frame, improving execution against existing parameters, becoming more skilled at a defined task) is legitimate and often essential. The surgeon who optimizes their technique saves lives. The athlete who optimizes their training wins. The manager who optimizes their communication produces better teams. None of that is in question. When the frame fits, optimization is the appropriate engagement and it produces real results.

The problem with optimization is specific: it cannot detect the errors that live at the level above it. It is designed to improve performance within a frame, which means it takes the frame as given. And when the frame is the problem (when the structure within which the optimization is occurring is what is generating the stuck), optimization not only fails to address the problem but actively obscures it.

Here is the mechanism of that obscuring. When someone is optimizing within a misaligned frame, they are producing visible evidence of improvement. The metrics move in the right direction. The execution becomes more refined. The effort produces measurable results. From the outside, and often from the inside, things appear to be working. The feedback is positive. The trajectory looks correct.

And underneath all of that visible improvement, the frame is being reinforced. Each successful optimization invests more deeply in the frame's organization of the situation. Each measurable gain makes the frame's parameters feel more like reality. The person becomes more committed to the direction they are improving in, at exactly the moment when what might serve them is a different direction entirely. The optimization is not wrong in itself. It is producing the wrong kind of certainty about a question that hasn't been asked.

This is why some of the most productive-looking people are stuck in ways that matter. Not because they are working on the wrong things in any obvious sense. Because they are optimizing within a frame that doesn't fit, and the optimization is making the mismatch harder to see. Success within the frame is masking the question of whether the frame still serves.

• • •

Orientation is different from optimization in a way that is precise and worth holding carefully.

Orientation asks not how to perform better within the existing structure, but whether the existing structure is the right one to be performing within. It is a question about position before it is a question about movement. It attends to the frame (to the assumptions being made about what is happening, what is available, what success means, what is at stake) before it attends to how well those assumptions are being acted on.

The word orientation is chosen deliberately. A person who is oriented knows where they are standing in relation to what matters. Not where they wish they were standing. Not where they think they should be standing. Where they actually are. That knowing (accurate, honest, without the distortion that urgency and assumption and habitual interpretation introduce) is the condition from which genuine movement becomes available.

Disorientation, by contrast, is the condition of acting from a frame that doesn't fit without knowing that the frame doesn't fit. The disoriented person is not failing to try. They are trying from a position that does not make the movement they want available, inside a structure that is organizing what they see in ways that prevent them from recognizing the mismatch. Their effort is real. Their commitment is genuine. Their position is wrong, in the specific sense that it is not the position from which what they need to do is possible.

Orientation restores the prior condition. It does not tell you what to do (that is what optimization is for, once the direction is sound). It tells you where you are, which is the information required before any question about what to do can be answered well.

• • •

There is a concern that arises naturally at this point, and it is worth naming directly because it is often what prevents people from asking the orientation question at all.

If I stop and ask where I'm standing instead of how to do this better, am I not just creating permission to avoid action? Is this not a philosophically sophisticated way of staying in my head instead of getting on with the thing?

The concern is understandable. We live in environments that treat reflection as a luxury and action as the only real currency. The instruction to stop and assess position before optimizing performance runs against the grain of almost everything that productivity culture reinforces. It looks, from inside a culture organized around output, like hesitation dressed up as wisdom.

But the concern confuses two different things. It confuses orientation (which is about establishing the ground from which action becomes possible) with deliberation, which is a form of staying in the head that can indeed become avoidance. These are not the same. Orientation is not extended analysis. It is not weighing more options or gathering more information or constructing more elaborate models of the situation. It is the simpler and harder thing of honestly attending to where you actually are, right now, in relation to what actually matters.

That honest attention is often brief. It does not replace action; it precedes it. And the action that follows from accurate orientation is qualitatively different from the action that follows from urgency and assumption. It is better aimed. It requires less force. It is more likely to reach the level where the actual problem lives, because it was directed from a position that could see where that level is.

The alternative (acting immediately and constantly from within the existing frame, optimizing against existing parameters without pausing to ask whether the parameters still serve) is not more productive. It is more busy. Those are not the same thing, and the difference between them is exactly what most exhausted, effortful, not-quite-arriving experience is made of.

• • •

What does orientation actually look like? Not as a practice or a technique, but as a quality of attention that can be brought to a situation that isn't working?

It looks like a particular kind of honesty about what is actually happening, as distinct from what the current frame says is happening. A willingness to hold the situation loosely enough to ask whether the way it is being organized is serving it: whether the definition of the problem, the measure of success, the sense of what is available and what isn't, is accurate to the actual conditions or an artifact of the frame through which those conditions are being perceived.

Some questions move in this direction. Not because they are a technique to apply, but because they attend to the right level. Is consistent effort in this direction producing the kind of movement I expected, or increasingly expensive versions of the same stuck? Is the way I am understanding this situation generating the problem, or responding to it? If I stepped back from the assumption that I know what this situation requires, what would I actually see? Am I improving within a frame that fits, or becoming more skilled at something that isn't working?

These are not comfortable questions. They require a willingness to hold uncertainty that optimization actively discourages: to sit with not knowing what to do next while the prior question of where you are is attended to. That discomfort is real. And the reluctance to sit with it is precisely why the orientation question so rarely arrives on its own. It takes something to ask it. Not courage in any grand sense, but a willingness to slow down inside a moment where everything is pushing for speed.

What it produces, when the attention is honest, is not a new plan. It is a shift in what is visible. The situation begins to look different. Options that were not accessible from within the old frame become apparent. The problem that seemed fixed and external begins to show its edges, the places where the frame is imposing a particular organization that the situation itself does not require. The direction that was obviously necessary begins to reveal itself as one choice among others rather than the only possible way forward.

That shift in what is visible is what orientation provides. It does not tell you what to do with what you now see. That is yours. But seeing accurately is the precondition for everything else: for the choice that doesn't require force, the commitment that can be held without continuous effort to maintain it, the movement that follows from a position that makes it genuinely available.

• • •

This chapter has been building to a simple formulation, simple enough to carry forward into the rest of the book and into whatever you are navigating that brought you here.

When things are not working: before asking how to do this better, ask where you are standing.

That is the question that changes everything. Not because it always produces an immediate answer. Not because asking it is comfortable or quick. But because it attends to the level where the actual problem most often lives: the level of the frame, the position, the organizational structure that is determining what seems possible before any assessment of how to proceed begins.

Once you can see where you are standing, the question of what to do becomes answerable in a way it was not before. Not prescribed (this book does not prescribe action, and the reason for that restraint will become fully apparent by the time the last chapter is reached). But answerable in the sense that the answer becomes visible, natural, obvious in the way that things become obvious when you are standing somewhere that makes them accessible.

The next chapter takes this reorientation into five specific areas of lived experience: five places where standing differently changes what becomes visible, and what becomes available, more than any refinement of technique within the existing frame could.

Why Effort Fails

9. Five Places This Shows Up In Your Life

Where the reframe changes what you see

The five chapters before this one built something. They built a structural account of why effort fails: of what a human being actually is, what a frame is and why you can't see yours, why harder doesn't help when the problem lives above the level where harder reaches, what stuck is actually telling you, and what question to ask instead of the one that's been making things worse. That account is now in your possession.

This chapter doesn't add to it. It applies it. Across five areas of lived experience where the reframe consistently changes the most, where what has been built in the preceding chapters, brought into contact with specific territory, makes things visible that weren't visible before.

These five areas are not arbitrary. They are where the structural dynamics this book describes most reliably show up in recognizable, daily, concrete form. They are also where the misapplication of effort (effort applied at the wrong level, from the wrong position, in the wrong direction) tends to concentrate and compound. The reader who has been following the book will find the territory familiar. What changes here is the resolution of the picture.

You may find that one of these five lands with particular force. That it describes something specific, something you have been inside, with a precision that the earlier chapters only gestured toward. That is the chapter working as it is meant to. Each of these domains is, in its own way, a place where the same underlying structure plays out. Recognizing it in yours is the point.

• • •

The first place the reframe changes things is the domain of agency: your actual, daily experience of making choices.

Or not making them. That is usually where the trouble shows up. You face a decision that has been available for longer than it should have been and that you cannot seem to close. Or you make a commitment and then watch yourself quietly fail to act on it, not from forgetting, not from changed circumstances, but from something that feels like the opposite of will: like the capacity to move in that direction simply isn't there. Or you decide, with genuine intention, and then reverse the decision three days later without being entirely sure why. Or you want something clearly and cannot bring yourself to choose it.

Before the reframe that this book has been building, all of this reads as a failure of agency. You should be able to decide. You should be able to commit. The gap between wanting something and moving toward it is a character gap: something insufficient in will, or clarity, or courage, or discipline. That reading is so automatic and so culturally reinforced that it rarely surfaces for inspection. It just arrives, as the obvious interpretation of the experience.

After the reframe, the same experience reads differently. Chapter 7 described what protective choosing actually is: the self-organizing system accurately reporting that no genuinely resourceful option is currently available from its current position. The inability to commit is not a malfunction. It is the system doing its job, refusing to make a commitment it cannot sustain, protecting a coherence that forced commitment would contradict.

What this changes in practice is the question you ask when commitment isn't available. The old question is what is wrong with me, and it points toward self-coercion: more discipline, more pressure, overriding the refusal and committing anyway. That approach produces a commitment the system cannot hold, which either collapses or requires continuous effort to maintain. The new question is what position would make a sustainable commitment available, and it points toward something genuinely different: not more force in the same direction, but attention to what the conditions actually are.

It also makes readable something you have almost certainly experienced but may not have had language for: the moment when a decision you couldn't make simply became obvious. Not because you resolved to decide. Not because you reasoned your way past the resistance. Because something in the conditions shifted, and what had been unavailable became available. The decision didn't feel forced. It felt clear. The person you were when you made it didn't feel stronger than the person who had been stuck. They were standing somewhere different.

That experience (and understanding what it actually is) changes the relationship to the interval before it. The period during which commitment isn't available is not wasted time accumulating evidence against your character. It is the system attending to what conditions actually support. The appropriate response to that interval is not always to wait, and not always to push. It is to understand what the system is reporting and to ask honestly what would need to shift for a genuinely resourceful option to become visible.

Sometimes that inquiry produces something actionable. Sometimes it produces the recognition that the conditions are not yet ready, and that patience is more accurate than pressure. Either way, the experience is now structural information rather than personal verdict. That shift in what the experience means is itself a change in position. And a change in position is, as the preceding chapters have established, what makes movement available when force cannot.

• • •

The second domain is leadership, which, for the purposes of this chapter, means any situation in which you are trying to influence the behavior of other people. Whether you hold a formal title or not.

The conventional model of influence is built on direction: tell people what to do clearly enough, hold them accountable firmly enough, and apply sufficient consequence to the gap between instruction and compliance. The model is so deeply embedded in most thinking about organizations and management that it barely appears as a model. It appears as common sense. Of course you get results by making expectations clear and consequences real.

Applied to what the preceding chapters have established about self-organizing systems, that model has a specific and predictable failure mode. Other people are also self-organizing systems. They respond to pressure not by simply receiving and transmitting it but by interpreting it, integrating what they can, resisting what they cannot. Compliance is available; engagement is not. The person who follows a directive under sufficient pressure will do what is required when the pressure is applied. They will not do it with the quality of judgment, initiative, and genuine investment that makes the difference between adequate performance and the kind of performance that actually matters. And when the pressure is removed (when the manager isn't watching, when the accountability structure relaxes, when the organizational moment passes), the behavior reverts. The embedded system reasserts its organization. The direction didn't reach.

This is why organizations that manage through authority and consequence often find themselves managing the same problems repeatedly. The problems are addressed at the surface. At the level where the actual organization of the system is maintained, nothing has shifted. The people inside the organization are doing what self-organizing systems do: protecting their coherence against pressure that they cannot integrate. The compliance is real and the engagement is absent, and the long-term result is a system that functions when directed and collapses when the direction is removed.

What actually influences self-organizing systems is different from direction, and it operates at a different level. Chapter 4 established that self-organizing systems respond to conditions. They reorganize when conditions shift in ways that make a different organization available. Influence, understood structurally, is the act of participating in those conditions in ways that make a different organization genuinely available to the systems you are working with.

That sounds abstract until you have watched it operate. What it looks like, in practice, is this: someone who stands clearly in relation to what matters, who responds to what is actually happening rather than to what they wish were happening, who maintains that position under pressure without rigidity, who can name what the situation actually requires without requiring others to pretend it requires something else, creates a kind of reference point. Not through authority. Through coherence. The systems around that person have something to orient themselves relative to. Something that is stable enough to trust and honest enough to be useful.

The influence this generates is qualitatively different from the compliance that direction produces. It is people thinking for themselves from a clearer position, rather than executing instructions from an unclear one. It is initiative that doesn't require instruction, because the direction is visible from where they are standing. It is engagement rather than compliance, which is to say, it is the kind of change that holds when the external pressure is removed, because it was organized from inside the system rather than imposed on it from outside.

For practitioners (coaches, therapists, consultants, teachers, anyone whose work involves supporting other people through change), this is the domain that most directly affects how the work operates. The question is not what technique to apply but what level the technique is reaching. A technique that operates at the level of behavior without reaching the frame that is organizing the behavior will produce results that are real and temporary: the behavior changes while the structural source of the behavior remains intact, and eventually the source reasserts itself. The question "where is this person standing?" (asked genuinely, not as a method) reaches the level where something that lasts can actually occur.

• • •

The third domain is time, which means something more specific than it might initially seem. Not time management, and not productivity. The domain of time, as this book means it, is your relationship to what has already happened and to what has not happened yet. To the past you are carrying and the future you can or cannot imagine.

Frames organize both. This is one of the less obvious but more consequential things a frame does. It does not only organize what you perceive in the present moment. It organizes what your history means, and it determines what futures seem available from where you are standing. The same sequence of events can be organized, by different frames, as evidence of a pattern that will persist or as evidence of conditions that have now changed. The same set of circumstances can feel like a path that is closed or a situation that is genuinely open. The difference is not in the events or the circumstances. It is in the frame through which they are being organized.

Temporal disorientation (the experience of being trapped in a past you cannot leave, or unable to imagine a genuine future, or disconnected from any sense of continuity between who you were and who you are now) is, in the structural account this book offers, a frame problem rather than a time problem. Something in the current frame is organizing the timeline in a way that produces these experiences. The past is not actually imprisoning you. A particular organization of the past is. And that organization, being a frame, is not visible as an organization. It looks like reality. The history you are carrying feels like the history, not one account of it among other possible accounts, but what actually happened and what it actually means.

What the reframe makes available here is a specific kind of inquiry. Not the instruction to be more positive about your history, or to visualize the future more vividly, or to reframe the past as a source of strength rather than a source of damage. Those instructions operate at the wrong level, as Chapter 5 established.

They try to change what you see without changing the structure through which you are seeing it.

The structural inquiry asks something different: how is the current frame organizing this timeline? What is it making necessary in the past: what does it require that events mean in order for its current organization to remain coherent? What is it foreclosing in the future: what options, what directions, what versions of what is possible have been excluded before the question of what to do even begins? These are not comfortable questions. They require a willingness to look at the structure of the story being told rather than just at its contents.

But they are questions that go somewhere. Unlike the instruction to feel differently about the past, which tries to overwrite a meaning structure through conscious intention, the structural inquiry attends to where the frame is organizing that structure and why. And when a frame's organization of time is seen clearly enough (when the particular way it is constructing the past and foreclosing the future becomes visible as a construction rather than as reality), something shifts that cannot be produced through any amount of positive reframing.

There is also an experience on the other side of this worth naming. The temporal reorganization that follows a genuine frame shift is one of the more striking things that happens in the process of real change. The history looks different, not because the events changed but because what they mean changed, and what they mean changed because the frame through which they were being organized changed. Experiences that were organized as evidence of a story that constrained you are now organized as part of a story that does not. This is not revision or distortion. It is the same accuracy that was always available from a different position. The events are intact. The organization of their meaning is new. And from the new organization, futures become imaginable that the old one had placed outside the frame.

• • •

The fourth domain is identity: who you understand yourself to be, and what happens to that understanding when the frame shifts.

The common account of identity treats it as something prior to experience: a core self that was there before, that persists through change, that is the stable substrate from which behavior and interpretation and relationship emerge. The language around this is everywhere. Finding yourself. Being true to yourself. Knowing who you really are. All of it assumes a fixed interior thing that the right circumstances or the right exploration will reveal.

The structural account this book offers is different. Identity, in this account, is not prior to experience. It is what has organized itself through experience: through how you have stood, acted, interpreted, and been shaped by what you navigated. It is residue rather than essence. Which means it is real and durable and genuinely yours, and also not fixed. It is the current organization of a self-organizing system. And as the preceding chapters have established, self-organizing systems reorganize when conditions shift in ways that make a different organization available.

This explains one of the more disorienting experiences that genuine change produces: the sense that you no longer quite recognize yourself. Ways of being that felt essential have become optional. Responses that seemed automatic have slowed down, become available for something other than automatic execution. Parts of you that were invisible (that were, perhaps, inconsistent with the frame's organization and so excluded from what felt like your self) have emerged. The person you were in the old frame and the person you are becoming in the new one are not the same, and the difference is not always comfortable.

This is not dissolution of self. It is what structural reorganization looks like in the domain of identity. And understanding it as structural rather than as a loss of something that was real and should have been permanent changes what the experience requires of you. It does not require you to hold on to the old identity in order to maintain continuity. It does not require you to grieve the aspects of yourself that are reorganizing as though you are losing them. It invites, instead, a kind of honest attention to what is actually emerging: to what the system is becoming as the frame shifts, which is often something that fits more accurately than what preceded it.

There is also a specific version of this that is worth naming directly, because it accounts for a great deal of the resistance that shows up when change is genuinely available. When the question "who am I if I'm not this?" arises (when the prospect of the frame shifting means that a substantial part of how you have understood yourself would reorganize), the response is often to hold the old frame in place through the sheer weight of identity investment. Not because the old frame serves. Because releasing it feels like releasing yourself. The threat is not to survival in any literal sense. It is to the continuity of an identity that has been organized around the frame that is no longer fitting.

The reframe that makes this workable is the one already implicit in the structural account: what you are is not identical to what you have been organized as. The self that would persist through a frame shift is not the same as the organization that a particular frame has produced. You are not your current organization any more than the system is its current state. You are the thing that organizes, and reorganizes, and continues through both. That recognition does not make the experience of identity reorganization comfortable. But it makes it navigable, which is different from requiring it not to happen.

• • •

The fifth domain is the one that is most often overlooked when the first four are going well, and the one that produces the most confusion when it isn't. It is the domain of the systems you are embedded in.

Every individual exists inside multiple systems simultaneously. Relationships with particular people, each organized around its own shared history and expectations. A family, which has its own coherence requirements and its own resistance to pressure it cannot integrate. An organization or workplace, with its own culture and the accumulated weight of how things are done here. A community, a culture, a set of institutions that organize what is normal and expected and available. You are not separate from these systems and they are not separate from you. You are, in part, constituted by them. The frame you operate from did not originate in isolation. It developed through contact with these systems and their own frames.

They are also self-organizing. This is the thing that matters most here, and the thing that is easiest to forget when personal change is going well. The systems you are embedded in have their own organization. They maintain that organization through the same mechanisms that any self-organizing system uses: through the accumulated weight of expectation, habit, shared meaning, and the resistance to pressure that cannot be integrated into the existing coherence. When you change in ways that those systems cannot integrate, they push back. Not because anyone in those systems has decided to resist you. Because the system is doing what systems do.

This accounts for something that many people who have done genuine internal work have experienced and been troubled by: the return of old patterns in familiar environments. The change that felt real and durable in the context where it occurred (in a workshop, or a period of reflection, or a sustained engagement with something that shifted the frame) quietly erodes when the person returns to the systems that were organized around the old frame. The workplace responds to them as though they are the person they were before. The family expects the same behaviors it has always expected. The relationships proceed according to the established organization. And the pressure to step back into the old position, distributed across all of these systems simultaneously, can be sufficient to produce reversion without any single event being identifiable as the cause.

Understanding this as structural rather than personal changes what it means. It is not evidence that the change was shallow. It is not evidence that the systems around you are hostile to your growth, though they may occasionally feel that way. It is the embedded system doing exactly what embedded systems do when they encounter pressure they cannot integrate: reasserting the organization that has the weight of history behind it. The appropriate response is not to fight the systems more forcefully, which is effort applied at the wrong level. It is to understand what the systems are organized around, what coherence they are maintaining, and what would be required for them to reorganize rather than resist.

Sometimes that inquiry reveals things that can be worked with: ways of introducing the new frame into the existing systems that allow them to integrate it rather than resist it, or recognizing which systems are genuinely incompatible with the change that has occurred and attending to that honestly. Sometimes it reveals that the environment is organized in ways that make the movement you want structurally unavailable regardless of what you do internally, that the constraint is not personal but positional, and that what is required is attention to position rather than intensified internal effort.

The practical implication is this: genuine individual change is often a necessary condition for the life to look different, but it is not a sufficient one. The systems you are embedded in will reorganize at their own pace, in response to conditions that include but are not limited to your own reorientation. Expecting them to respond immediately, or interpreting their failure to respond immediately as evidence that your own change wasn't real, applies the wrong standard to the wrong level. You changed. The systems are still organized around who you were. Those two things can both be true simultaneously, and navigating the gap between them is itself part of what working at the right level requires.

• • •

Five domains. Five places where the same structural account (the one built across the preceding chapters) produces different things becoming visible when it is brought into contact with specific territory.

The reason the chapter is built the way it is (one domain at a time, with each one given enough room to become concrete) is that the reframe lands differently in different lives. Some readers will have found the agency domain describing something they have been living with for years. Others will have recognized themselves most clearly in the identity section, or the systems section, or the account of time. The structural dynamics are the same across all five. The experience of recognition tends to arrive through the domain that fits most precisely.

What all five domains share is this: in each one, the shift from asking what is wrong with me to asking where am I standing is the move that changes what is available. Not because standing somewhere different is easy, or immediate, or something that follows automatically from understanding that position matters. But because the question that correctly locates the problem is the question from which a useful answer can actually emerge.

Chapter 10 takes up what happens after that answer begins to arrive, after a genuine frame shift occurs, and the work of living inside the new frame begins. That chapter is the one most books about change do not include. It addresses the specific things that happen in the aftermath of real reorganization, and why they are not what they usually look like.

10. After the Shift

What happens when something genuine reorganizes, and why it sometimes fades

Most books about change end when the change happens. The insight arrives, the frame shifts, the stuck resolves, and the book closes on that note. The reader is left with the breakthrough and no account of what comes next. This chapter is what comes next.

It is the chapter that most books about change do not include, because including it would require acknowledging something those books are not structured to acknowledge: that genuine reorganization does not arrive fully formed, stable, and permanent. It arrives incomplete. It arrives surrounded by systems that have not yet reorganized. It arrives needing something that cannot be hurried and that is easy to mistake for the absence of progress. This chapter is an account of that interval: what it is, why it looks the way it looks, and what it actually requires.

The reader this chapter most directly addresses is one who has done real work. Who has understood something at a level that felt genuine, not merely intellectual. Who has experienced the shift: the moment when the frame changed and the situation looked different and the stuck that had been organizing experience simply wasn't there in the same way. And who has then watched, with confusion or discouragement, as that clarity gradually eroded. As the old patterns reasserted themselves. As the insight that seemed so solid became something remembered rather than inhabited.

That experience is not evidence that the insight was shallow. It is not evidence that you failed to commit to it, or that the shift wasn't real, or that you are the kind of person who understands things but cannot hold them. It is a structural phenomenon with a specific account, and understanding that account changes the relationship to what is happening.

· · ·

Consider what a frame shift actually is, and what it is not.

A frame shift is a reorganization of the structure through which experience is organized. Chapter 5 established what frames are and how they work: not perspectives consciously adopted, but structures that organize what seems possible, necessary, and constrained before conscious interpretation begins. When a frame shifts, that organizational structure changes. What was invisible becomes visible. What seemed fixed reveals itself as a current state rather than a permanent condition. The situation that felt closed begins to show openings that were always there and simply could not be seen from the previous position.

This is a real change. It is not a cognitive reframing in the shallow sense: not a decision to look at things differently while the underlying structure remains unchanged. Something in the organizational structure itself has moved. The perception is different because the structure producing it is different.

But that change has a specific scope. What shifted is the frame. What has not yet shifted, at the moment of the shift, is everything that the frame was organizing. The habitual responses built up across years of operating from the old frame. The emotional associations: the cues that trigger familiar patterns automatically, before conscious processing has a chance to intervene. The behavioral defaults: the way you respond to conflict, or to uncertainty, or to being evaluated, or to the specific situations that have been organized most heavily by the old frame. The self-concept: the accumulated story of who you are, which was assembled largely under the old frame's organizational influence and which still carries its shape.

None of these reorganize in the moment of the frame shift. They are downstream of the frame. They are, in a sense, the deposits the old frame left behind: the residue of years of perception organized in a particular way, expressed in behavior, emotional response, and self-understanding that are now organized around a frame that is no longer operating as it was. The shift happened at the level of the structure. The patterns that the structure produced are still in place, still running, still generating the responses they were built to generate.

This is why the insight fades. It is not that the insight disappears. It is that the system built around the old frame continues operating, and the familiar conditions that activate those old patterns (the conversation that always produces a particular response, the environment that always triggers a particular contraction, the relationship that has always organized itself around a particular dynamic) are still there. They activate what they have always activated. The new frame is present as understanding, but it has not yet propagated into the patterns that daily life is largely made of. And when those patterns activate, it is easy to conclude that nothing changed, because the surface behavior (the response that arrived before reflection could intervene) is recognizably the old one.

The frame shifted. The patterns are catching up. That is what is happening. It is not failure.

• • •

There is a more specific version of this worth naming, because it produces a particular quality of discouragement that can be difficult to navigate without understanding what it actually is.

Reversion is what happens when the embedded systems of a person's life push back against the new organization and the old frame reasserts itself, not as a deliberate return but as a structural response to accumulated pressure. It is distinct from ordinary backsliding: a lapse in behavior that the person notices and corrects. Reversion is a fuller return: a period during which the new orientation is largely absent, replaced by something that feels like the old organization operating with its full weight.

What produces it is the pressure of the embedded systems that Chapter 9 described. The people who know you and have organized their relationship to you around the old frame. The role or environment that was built to fit the person you were before the shift. The internal patterns (habitual response, emotional association, behavioral default) that are organized around the old structure and that activate with enough force, under enough familiar pressure, to override the new frame temporarily. None of this is chosen. It happens below the level of decision. One day the new frame is present and accessible, and then the right combination of circumstances arrives, and something that felt like a new organization has simply been replaced by the old one.

Before understanding reversion structurally, most people interpret it as evidence that they are not the kind of person who can hold what they understand. The insight was real, but they (specifically they, with their particular inadequacy in this domain) could not sustain it. This interpretation is not only incorrect. It is actively counterproductive, because it adds the weight of self-recrimination to the structural pressure already present, making the return to the new orientation harder rather than easier.

The structural interpretation is different. The embedded system exerted pressure. The new organization, which has not yet fully propagated through the patterns of daily life and has not yet had time to become the weight-bearing structure, gave way. This is what self-organizing systems do under pressure that they cannot yet fully integrate: they revert to the organization that has the most history behind it. It is not a verdict on character. It is a temporary reassertion of the prior structure in response to conditions it is still built to navigate.

Understanding reversion this way changes what is available in its aftermath. You can return to the new orientation without first establishing, through an extended episode of self-recrimination, that you are the problem. The new orientation is still there. The frame shift was real. What happened was structural and temporary and workable. You can simply pick up the thread.

• • •

Integration is what the self-organizing system does, in its own time and at its own pace, after a genuine frame shift has occurred. It is the process by which the shift propagates from the level of the frame into the downstream patterns (the habitual responses, the emotional associations, the behavioral defaults, the self-concept) that were organized under the old frame and are now, gradually, reorganizing themselves to fit the new one.

This process does not look like anything in particular from the outside. It is largely invisible. There is no metric for it. There is no visible behavior that indicates it is proceeding, no clear marker that distinguishes the integration interval from stagnation. To observation (including the person's own self-observation), it can appear that nothing is happening at all. The frame shift occurred, something changed, and now the days are proceeding without obvious evidence that the change is deepening or stabilizing. The person is still responding to familiar situations with familiar patterns. The new frame is accessible in reflection but not always present in the moment. Progress, if there is progress, is happening somewhere below the threshold of conscious observation.

This is how integration works. It is not a process that can be observed directly while it is occurring. It is recognized mostly in retrospect: looking back, something that was difficult no longer is. A response that was automatic has slowed down. A pattern that seemed permanent has lost its grip. The change is not visible as it happens. It is visible as what is now available that was not available before.

The crucial fact about integration is that it cannot be forced. This is worth holding carefully, because everything about the way most people are organized around effort will push toward forcing it. You understand something. The understanding feels important. You want it to be stable, permanent, fully realized. You want to install it. To make sure it holds. To do the work that will consolidate the shift and protect it from erosion. And all of that wanting (all of that urgent engagement with the new frame as something to be managed and maintained and enforced against the possibility of reversion) tends to interrupt exactly the process it is trying to protect.

Integration is what a self-organizing system does when left to its own timing after reorganization occurs. The system is not passive in this process (it is doing real work, redistributing the weight of the new organization through its interconnected patterns, adjusting emotional associations, rewriting behavioral defaults slowly enough that the coherence of the whole is maintained). But it is doing this work at the level where it actually needs to happen, which is not the level where conscious effort operates. Conscious effort applied to the integration process doesn't accelerate it. It occupies the territory where the integration is occurring and substitutes intentional management for the organic process that was already proceeding.

The analogy that is most accurate here is not anything about personal development. It is biological. When tissue repairs itself after injury, the repair proceeds at the rate the biology requires. Applying force to speed the process does not accelerate the repair. It disrupts the conditions under which the repair is occurring. The appropriate response to healing is not management but protection: creating the conditions in which the process can proceed without interference. Integration after a frame shift works analogously. The system is repairing its own coherence around the new organization. The appropriate response is not to manage the repair but to protect the conditions in which it can proceed.

$$\bullet \ \bullet \ \bullet$$

There is a specific interval in the integration process that is worth describing with some precision, because it is the place where most people abandon the new orientation under the mistaken belief that it has failed.

It comes after the initial shift, and after the first flush of clarity that often accompanies a genuine frame change. The new frame is real: the person is not imagining that something has changed. But the change is not yet stable. It is not yet the operating organization of daily life. It is present in certain contexts and absent in others, accessible in reflection and sometimes inaccessible in the moment, available in some relationships and crowded out in others where the old dynamic is still running. The person is, in the language Chapter 6 introduced, in a transformational process that is not moving at a translational pace. Nothing visible is happening. The old patterns are still present. The new frame is real but intermittent.

This interval looks, from the inside and often from the outside, like stagnation. Like having been close to something and then losing it. Like a plateau or a regression. The natural response to that appearance is to intervene: to push, to examine what went wrong, to apply more effort in the direction of the new frame. To decide that if nothing visible is happening then something invisible must be failing, and to do something about it.

That intervention is exactly the wrong response. Not because doing nothing is always right, but because what is being identified as stagnation is not stagnation. It is the integration interval: the period in which the self-organizing system is doing the work of distributing the new organization through its patterns at the rate that the patterns can absorb it. The work is real and it is proceeding. It simply does not produce visible output at the rate that translational progress does, because it is not a translational process. It is a reorganization. And reorganizations do not produce steady, measurable, linear progress toward completion. They proceed unevenly, invisibly, and according to the timing of the system rather than the impatience of the person watching.

The most common mistake in this interval is to reintroduce translational effort into a transformational process. To decide that since the new understanding isn't yet fully installed, the solution is to work harder at installing it: to reflect more, process more, apply the new frame more deliberately, track compliance with the new organization more vigilantly. This produces a specific and recognizable outcome: the new frame becomes a project to be managed rather than an orientation to be inhabited. It becomes effortful in the way that the old wrong-level efforts were effortful. And the effort itself signals to the system that something is fragile and under threat, which activates the protective responses that make stability harder rather than easier to achieve.

The better response to the integration interval is not more effort. It is accurate recognition: this is what the interval looks like, and it does not mean what it appears to mean. Reduce the pressure. Maintain orientation: remain available to the new frame when it is accessible, without requiring it to be dominant when it is not. Trust that the process is proceeding at a level below where observation reaches. And do not confuse the absence of visible progress with the absence of progress.

• • •

The quality of attention that supports integration has a particular character that is worth describing carefully, because it is easily mistaken for its opposite.

It might be called holding without gripping. It is remaining present to the new frame (available to see through it, available to operate from it, aware of what it makes visible) without converting that availability into vigilance. Without treating the new frame as something that needs to be actively maintained against the possibility of erosion. Without checking, repeatedly, whether the shift is still present. Without requiring the new orientation to be constantly accessible as proof that it was real.

Gripping is what happens when the relationship to the new frame becomes anxious. When the person is not just available to the new organization but working to enforce it, managing every response against the standard of the new frame, noticing every reversion with alarm, treating the integration process as something that could fail if vigilance lapses. This is a recognizable pattern and it is understandable: the shift felt important, the old organization was costly, the idea of losing what was gained is genuinely threatening. The grip is an attempt to protect something real.

But gripping converts the frame from something to see through into something to manage. It makes the new organization into an object of attention rather than a condition of perception. And that conversion interrupts the integration process that the grip is trying to protect. The self-organizing system cannot reorganize around an orientation that the person is simultaneously managing as a fragile possession. The management itself is a form of holding the system in a state of alert that is incompatible with the settled, distributed reorganization that integration requires.

Holding without gripping is a different relationship to the same thing. It is the willingness to trust that what shifted is real without requiring constant verification of its presence. It is remaining available to the new frame while also remaining available to the patterns that are still running from the old one, not as failures to be corrected but as the normal texture of a system in process. It is allowing the integration to proceed at the pace it proceeds, without either abandoning the new orientation in frustration or gripping it in anxiety. It is, in a sense, the integration interval's version of the orientation question: attending to where you actually are rather than to where you wish you were, or fear you might no longer be.

This quality of attention is not passive. It requires something real: the willingness to tolerate an interval during which the new frame is not yet fully stable, and to tolerate that without either forcing it to stabilize faster or concluding that its instability means it was never real. That tolerance is, in practice, the main work of the integration interval. Not action. Not management. The steadiness of a relationship to change that allows change to proceed.

• • •

The integration interval ends. This is worth saying plainly, because during it, the ending can be difficult to believe in.

What stabilization looks like is not a moment of arrival. It is not an announcement or a clear transition from unstable to stable. It is more like noticing, at some point, that the old pattern is no longer the automatic response to a situation that used to activate it reliably. That a response which always arrived without reflection now arrives with a slight delay, a moment of genuine choice, a different option visible where before there was only the one. That a relationship which always organized itself around a particular dynamic has quietly reorganized, and neither party quite knows when that happened.

The new frame does not replace the old one entirely. The old organization does not disappear. It is still available, especially under pressure, especially when the conditions that built it are strongly present. What changes is its weight. It no longer has the automatic authority it had. It is one organization among others rather than the default that everything returns to. And the new frame, which began as something present in reflection and intermittent in the moment, gradually becomes more reliably the operating structure: the thing that is doing the organizing before conscious interpretation begins.

This is what genuine change looks like in a self-organizing system. Not a dramatic replacement of one structure by another. A gradual shift in which organization changes weight, old patterns lose their automatic authority, new patterns gain it, and the person looks back after some interval and recognizes that something that was difficult is no longer difficult in the same way. It happened below observation. It required no management at the level where it occurred. What it required was protection of the conditions in which it could proceed, which meant, mainly, not applying translational effort to a transformational process, not gripping what needed to be held, and not interpreting the integration interval as failure.

Chapter 11 extends the account to the experience of working with others who are in these processes: to what it means to be in the position of trying to influence or support another person's movement, and why understanding what that person is actually navigating changes what genuine help requires.

11. What This Means For How You Work With Others

Systems, influence, and the practitioner's real work

Everything this book has covered applies to your own experience of effort, stuck, and change. This chapter applies it to the experience of working with other people who are stuck: to what you are actually doing when you sit across from someone who is not moving, and to how understanding what they are actually navigating changes what you can do about it.

This chapter is for practitioners in the broadest sense. Coaches and therapists, obviously. But also consultants, teachers, leaders, managers, parents: anyone who regularly finds themselves in the position of trying to help another human being move through something that isn't moving. The specific context varies enormously. The structural situation is the same in all of them: you are working with a self-organizing system, and whether or not you have understood it as such is one of the things that most determines what your work can reach.

What follows is not a new method. The field this book draws on does not prescribe technique, and this chapter will not break that restraint. What it offers is a structural account of what is happening in the work you are already doing: an account that, for many practitioners, will explain things they have already noticed in their best sessions without having had language for what made them different.

. . .

The foundational reframe this book introduced in Chapter 4 applies as directly to your practice as it does to your own life.

When you work with another person who is stuck, you are not working with a mechanism that needs repair. You are not diagnosing a malfunction, identifying the broken part, and applying the correct intervention to restore proper function. The mechanical model is as thoroughly embedded in most practitioner training as it is in everyday thinking about change, and it produces the same failure mode in professional practice that it produces in personal life: effort applied at the wrong level, from the wrong understanding of what the problem actually is.

What you are working with is a self-organizing system that is accurately responding to its current organization. The stuck is not malfunction. It is structural accuracy. The person sitting across from you is standing somewhere from which the movement they want is not currently available, and they are correctly reporting that condition. The system is not broken. It is organized in a way that does not, from its current position, make the movement available. Those are different situations, and they require different kinds of engagement.

The person who is trying harder and arriving nowhere is not failing. They are applying force to a system that cannot be moved through force at that level. The person who understands something in a session and then finds it gone by the following week is not uncommitted. The shift was real and the patterns built under the old organization are still running, which is exactly what Chapter 10 described. The person who cannot commit to a direction that seems obviously available from the outside is not avoidant. The system is accurately reporting that no genuinely resourceful option is visible from its current position.

In each case, the accurate description of what is happening is also the beginning of the accurate description of what the work actually is. Not: identify the deficiency and apply the correction. But: understand what the system's current organization is telling you, and attend to the conditions under which that organization might shift. That is a different kind of engagement. And it is one that most practitioner training does not prepare people for, because most practitioner training is built on the mechanical model and its assumptions about where change is located and how it occurs.

• • •

Most practitioners have had the experience of a technique that reliably works stopping working. Not with everyone: with particular people, or in particular periods of a relationship, or with a particular kind of presenting situation. The tool that has produced real movement a hundred times produces nothing. The approach that the practitioner has reason to trust falls flat. Something is clearly not reaching, and it is not obvious why.

The structural account is this: techniques operate within frames. They are designed to address problems as those problems are defined within a particular way of understanding what is happening. A technique for shifting a behavioral pattern assumes the pattern is the level where the problem lives. A technique for restructuring a thought assumes cognition is the level where the problem lives. A technique for accessing a buried emotion assumes affect is the level where the problem lives. All of these are sometimes right, and when they are right, the technique reaches and something moves.

When the frame itself is the problem (when the person's organization of their situation is what is generating the stuck), technique applied within the existing frame cannot reach it. Not because the technique is poor. Because it is operating at the wrong level. It is attempting to adjust the contents of a frame without touching the frame, and the frame is what is determining what the contents mean, what options are visible, what movements are available. You can shift a behavior, a thought, and an emotion within a frame that doesn't fit, and find that the frame reasserts each of them in its own terms before the next session.

This is not a criticism of technique. Technique is legitimate and often essential. The surgeon who operates skillfully saves the life that needed surgery. The question is whether surgery is what the situation requires: whether the level at which the technique is operating is the level where the problem actually lives. When those align, technique is the right engagement and it produces real results. When they don't align, more refined technique in the same direction produces more refined stuck.

Practitioners who have been working long enough have usually developed some felt sense of this distinction, even without language for it. There is a quality to the sessions where the tool is reaching that is different from the quality of sessions where something is being worked but the work isn't arriving anywhere. The person is engaged, the practitioner is competent, and somehow the level where the real problem lives is not being contacted. That felt sense is reliable. What is often missing is the structural account of what it is sensing: an account that makes it possible to orient toward the level where contact would actually occur, rather than simply recognizing that the current level is not it.

• • •

The conventional model of influence in practitioner work is directional: the practitioner knows what direction the person should move, and the work consists of helping them move in that direction. The specific means vary (some practitioners are more directive, some less; some use structured tools, some work more fluidly), but the underlying logic is similar. There is a destination, the practitioner can see it, and the work is a form of guided travel toward it.

Applied to self-organizing systems, this model has a specific and predictable failure mode that Chapter 9 described in the leadership domain. Directing a self-organizing system toward a predetermined destination produces compliance when the direction is present and reversion when it is removed. The system has not reorganized; it has been temporarily overridden. And because the override required force, and force in a self-organizing system is interpreted as pressure to be resisted, the reversion is often accompanied by a strengthening of the pattern that was being overridden. The practitioner has produced visible movement and invisible entrenchment simultaneously.

The alternative operates at a different level. It might be called influence through coherent standing: the practitioner is present to what is actually happening in the system (what the person's current organization is, what it is protecting, what it is accurately reporting) and responds to what is actually there rather than to what the practitioner has decided should be there. The practitioner is not directing the system toward a destination. They are attending to the conditions under which the system's own reorganization might become available.

This sounds like restraint, and it is. But it is not passivity. It is a more demanding and more effective form of engagement than direction, and the reason it is more effective is structural. Self-organizing systems reorganize in response to conditions. They do not reorganize in response to commands, however skillfully delivered. A practitioner who creates conditions (through the quality of their attention, through what they name and what they leave unnamed, through what they remain steady with and what they don't require to resolve) is working at the level where reorganization actually occurs. A practitioner who directs is working at a level the system can comply with without reorganizing.

The most consistent marker of this quality of influence is that the person in the session is doing the real work. Not performing understanding for the practitioner's benefit. Not generating the responses that the practitioner's frame has organized as the signs of progress. Actually working: following something into territory that the frame would not normally allow, staying with discomfort that the old organization would have resolved through one of its familiar routes, finding something that is genuinely their own rather than a version of what the practitioner's model predicted they would find. When that is happening, the practitioner has created conditions in which the system can do what self-organizing systems do when conditions support it. The influence is real. It is not visible as influence, because it is not operating as direction. It is operating as participation in the conditions that made the movement available.

Practitioners who have experienced this in their best sessions will recognize the description. There is something that happens when you stop trying to produce a specific outcome and start attending to what is actually present. The session changes quality. The person goes somewhere they might not have gone if the practitioner had been steering. Something arrives that the practitioner could not have predicted or directed toward, because it came from the system's own organization rather than from the practitioner's model of where the system should go. That is not accident or chemistry. It is accurate engagement with how self-organizing systems actually move.

• • •

The practical question that follows from all of this is not how to apply influence without command as a technique. It is what changes in the quality of attention that makes this kind of engagement possible.

The shift is from attending to content (what the person is saying, what it means, what it indicates about the problem and its resolution) to attending to organization. What is the frame that is organizing what this person is able to say and not say? What does the stuck tell you about where the system is standing? What is the system protecting through the resistance, and is that protection still serving the function it was built to serve? What are the conditions under which a different organization might become available?

These are not questions you ask the person, at least not directly. They are the questions you hold while you listen: the orientation from which you are attending. And that orientation changes what you hear. When you are attending to content, you hear the story. When you are attending to organization, you hear the frame that is telling the story: the assumptions about what is fixed and what is changeable, the meanings that have been settled without being examined, the places where the person's account of their own situation has edges that are slightly too clean. Those edges are where the frame is maintaining itself. They are also, often, where the system is closest to the instability that makes a shift possible.

Reversion, when it happens between sessions, reads differently through this lens. It is not evidence that the work is not progressing. It is structural information about the embedded systems that are organized around the old frame and are exerting the pressure that Chapter 10 described. What is worth attending to is not the reversion itself but what it reveals about the organization: which conditions triggered it, which embedded systems are organized most heavily around the old frame, where the new orientation is most vulnerable to being crowded out. That information is useful. The interpretation that reversion means failure is not.

The integration interval (the period after a genuine shift when nothing visible seems to be happening) is readable from outside the system in a way it often is not from inside it. A practitioner who understands what the integration interval is and what it looks like can recognize it when it appears, and can hold steady with it rather than intervening in ways that interrupt the process. That steadiness is itself a condition that supports integration. The person who is in the interval and anxious about its apparent stagnation is somewhat steadied by a practitioner who is not anxious about it, who can say, with genuine rather than performed confidence, that what is happening is what it should look like right now. That reassurance is only available to someone who actually understands what is happening and is not pretending calm in order to manage the person's distress.

• • •

There is a dimension of this chapter that is worth naming directly, even though it is the kind of claim that is easy to dismiss as imprecise.

A practitioner who has genuinely moved through the territory this book describes, who has experienced what frame-level reorganization feels like from the inside, who has felt the difference between effort applied at the wrong level and engagement that actually reaches where the problem lives, who has been through the integration interval themselves and recognized it for what it was, brings something to their work that training cannot provide and cannot fully substitute for. They know the territory from the inside.

This matters in practice. Not because shared experience creates automatic understanding (it does not). But because having inhabited the specific disorientation of genuine reorganization changes the practitioner's relationship to it in someone else. The impulse to resolve the disorientation quickly, to move the person past the uncomfortable interval, to produce visible progress when the process is in a period of invisible progress: that impulse is weaker in someone who has learned, through their own experience, that the disorientation is not a problem to be solved. It is a condition to be accompanied.

The practitioner who has experienced protective choosing in their own life sits differently with a person who cannot commit. They are not waiting for the commitment to arrive so the real work can begin. They understand that the inability to commit is the real work: that it is the system accurately reporting its current organization, and that attending to that report is more useful than managing the person toward a commitment they cannot yet sustain. That understanding comes from having been in the position themselves. It cannot be fully installed through training. It can only be recognized, through training, in practitioners who have already had it.

Similarly, the practitioner who has experienced reversion without interpreting it as personal failure sits differently with a client who has reverted. They do not communicate, explicitly or implicitly, that something has gone wrong that needs to be corrected. They can receive the reversion as structural information without adding the weight of disappointment to the structural pressure the person is already navigating. They can ask what conditions produced it (genuinely, from curiosity rather than from a framework that requires the person to have done something wrong), and that question reaches differently than the same question asked from a practitioner who is managing their own disappointment at the setback.

The shift the practitioner has made is, in this way, not separate from the shift that becomes available to the people they work with. It is the same shift, encountered in a different context and from a different position. And having inhabited it changes the quality of the company the practitioner can offer to someone who is in the middle of it, not yet through, not yet stable, but genuinely in motion at the level where motion actually occurs.

• • •

This is the practical upshot of everything the book has built: when you understand what you are actually working with, the nature of the work changes.

Not the tools necessarily, though some tools will reach differently than they did. Not the structure of the sessions, though some of what was structured to produce visible progress may need to make room for a different relationship to progress. What changes is the orientation from which you bring yourself to the work. The question you are holding when you listen. The things you can remain steady with that you previously needed to resolve. The quality of presence you can offer someone who is in a process that looks like stagnation and is not.

Agency without command is what influence looks like in a self-organizing system when it is working correctly. Not direction.

Not the application of a model to a problem. Participation: genuine contact with what is actually present in the system, responsive to what is actually happening rather than to what the practitioner's frame has organized as what should be happening. That participation, when it is real, creates conditions. And conditions are what self-organizing systems reorganize in response to. Not force. Not technique at the wrong level. The right conditions, offered with sufficient steadiness to allow the process its time.

Chapter 12 closes the book with a portrait of the reader on the other side of this reframe, not as a practitioner specifically, but as a person who has inhabited what these chapters have described. What life looks and feels like when the shift has landed, when effort is located where it can reach, when stuck is readable and reversion is navigable and movement is available in the specific way it becomes available when position is accurate. That portrait is what this book has been aimed at throughout. It is where all of this arrives.

12. What It Looks Like When It Works

A portrait of the reader on the other side

This chapter is not a summary. It does not review what the book has argued or collect the ideas into a tidy architecture. If you have arrived here having read what came before, you already have the argument. What this chapter offers is something different: a description of what it looks like and feels like when the argument has actually landed. Not in ideal form. Not all at once. But enough that the quality of engagement with your own life has shifted in the specific ways this book has been describing.

The portrait that follows is composite. It is not drawn from a single person or a single situation. It is an account of the recurring qualities of experience that emerge when the frame fits, when agency is coherent, when effort is located at the level where it can actually reach. These qualities are not dramatic. They are not the end of difficulty. They are something more modest and more durable than that: a different relationship to the difficulty that remains.

You may recognize some of this portrait already. You may recognize parts of it from moments in your own experience: times when something was working in this way before you had language for what was different. You may recognize almost none of it yet. Both of those are fine starting places. The portrait is not a test of how far along you are. It is a description of what is available on the other side of the reframe this book has been building.

• • •

Effort, on the other side of this reframe, feels proportionate.

Not easy. Not without cost. Not free of the ordinary demands that a life in motion makes on attention and energy. But proportionate: what the situation actually requires is roughly what you find yourself spending. The chronic surplus (the additional pressure applied inward, the self-coercion that kept things moving at the cost of a kind of ongoing exhaustion that was simply accepted as normal) is no longer a constant feature of the landscape.

This changes something that is hard to describe to someone who hasn't felt it shift. The exhaustion that comes from working against your own system's organization (from forcing commitment the system cannot sustain, from applying translational effort to situations that require transformation, from treating resistance as something to overcome rather than information to read) is a particular kind of tired. It does not resolve through rest alone, because it is structural rather than physical. It comes back on Monday whether or not the weekend was long enough, because it is not the consequence of effort; it is the consequence of effort applied from the wrong position.

When that structural mismatch resolves, something lifts that you may not have realized had weight. You notice it first in the quality of the effort that remains. There is still work. There are still tasks that are harder than others, still days when the energy isn't there, still commitments that require something real. But the effort has a different texture: it lands somewhere rather than absorbing into resistance. You are not pushing against yourself. The system is not fighting the direction. The cost is the actual cost, not the actual cost plus the overhead of self-coercion.

This proportionality is not a permanent state. Misalignment reasserts itself: new situations, new pressures, new frames settling into place that may not fit. What changes is not that proportionate effort is always present but that disproportionate effort is now recognizable when it appears. You notice when you are spending more than the situation requires. And that noticing is itself the beginning of the reorientation question: not what's wrong with me, but where am I standing, and is this position making more effort necessary than the actual work demands?

· · ·

When movement isn't available, it reads differently.

The experience of stuck (of pressing against something that won't give, of effort that produces no corresponding motion) does not disappear on the other side of this reframe. Stuck is still uncomfortable. It still carries its own particular quality of frustration. These things do not change.

What changes is what the discomfort points toward. Before the reframe, stuck was legible primarily as information about the person in the stuck. You weren't moving because something was wrong with you: your motivation wasn't sufficient, your commitment wasn't real, your character was deficient in some relevant way. The stuck was a verdict, and the discomfort of stuck was the discomfort of sitting with an unfavorable verdict about yourself while trying to figure out how to overturn it.

After the reframe, stuck reads as structural information. Something about position is making the movement in question unavailable. The question that arises is not what's wrong with me but where am I standing. That is a different question in a specific and important way: it is a question that can be engaged. You can look at position. You can attend to what the frame is organizing and whether that organization fits the actual situation. You can ask what the system might be protecting and whether that protection is still required. These are inquiries that go somewhere. A verdict on character mostly doesn't.

This shift does not make stuck pleasant. But it makes it workable in a way it wasn't before. The discomfort no longer has to be suppressed or overcome or argued with; it can be received as pointing toward something specific. Where is the resistance? What is the frame organizing? Is what seems constrained actually constrained, or does it appear constrained from a particular position that could change?

Sometimes the inquiry reveals that the stuck is appropriate: that the conditions genuinely don't support the movement, that what was needed was to understand this rather than to force past it. Sometimes it reveals that the frame itself is what was generating the immovability, and that a shift in position makes available what effort within the old frame could not. Either way, the experience is information now, not indictment. That alone changes what is possible.

· · ·

There are situations in which commitment is not available. You face an option (a direction, a change, a choice that seems like it should be obvious) and you cannot bring yourself to move toward it. Not from indifference. Not from failure of will. Something in you simply will not commit, and the more you try to press past that refusal, the more resistant it becomes.

Before the reframe, this experience was almost universally interpreted as a failure of character. You should be able to choose. Other people seem to choose. The inability to commit (when the stakes are clear and the direction is apparently obvious) registers as something wrong with you: weakness, fear, avoidance dressed up as deliberation.

The reframe this book has offered is different. When commitment isn't available, the self-organizing system is accurately reporting that no genuinely resourceful option is currently visible from its current position. The inability to commit is not a malfunction. It is the system protecting coherence: refusing to make a commitment that would require it to contradict its own organization in ways it cannot sustain. That protection is not the enemy of good decision-making. It is, in its way, the system doing its job.

On the other side of this reframe, the experience of not being able to commit to a particular option no longer automatically reads as a verdict on character. It reads as structural information. Something about the current position makes no genuinely resourceful choice visible in this direction. The question is not how to force commitment but what conditions might need to shift so that a choice that the system can actually sustain becomes available.

This is a quieter experience than the one it replaces, and that quietness is part of what takes getting used to. The urgency to override the refusal and commit anyway (the sense that willpower is what's missing and more of it would solve the problem) is replaced by something slower and less dramatic: an attention to what the conditions actually are and what they actually require. The interval during which commitment isn't available becomes a period of attending rather than an indictment accumulating toward a conclusion about who you are.

It is worth being honest that this is not always comfortable either. The world around a person who is in protective choosing often does not share the structural interpretation of what is happening. The pressure to decide, to commit, to act, continues from outside even when the conditions inside do not support it. What changes is not that pressure; it is what you make of your own experience of not being able to comply with it. That internal shift (from self-indictment to structural attending) does not remove the external pressure but it changes what you are carrying while you navigate it.

• • •

The embedded systems of life push back. This is not a failure of the reframe; it is one of the things the reframe predicts.

You understand something. The frame shifts. The position changes. Something that felt fixed becomes workable, and for a time you are operating from the new orientation with a quality of engagement that is recognizably different. And then something happens (pressure, fatigue, an old context reasserting itself, a familiar set of circumstances that the prior frame was built to navigate) and you find yourself back in the old organization. The insight seems to have evaporated. The shift seems not to have held. You are, in some identifiable way, somewhere you thought you had left.

Before the reframe, this experience had a reliable interpretation: you failed. You didn't hold it. You had the understanding and lost it, which means either the understanding wasn't real or you weren't the kind of person who could keep it. The reversion became evidence accumulating against you.

The reframe offers a different account, and this account matters because reversion is normal. The embedded system exerted pressure (as embedded systems do) and the new orientation, which has not yet had time to become the embedded organization, gave way to the older pattern. This is not failure. It is the self-organizing system doing what self-organizing systems do: maintaining the organization that has the weight of history behind it when conditions push in that direction. The frame didn't collapse. The system reasserted the prior organization under pressure. Those are different things.

On the other side of this reframe, reversion does not carry the additional weight of having failed to hold what you understood. The understanding is still there. The new orientation is still available. What happened was structural, not a referendum on whether the change was real. You can return to the new position without first serving a sentence of self-recrimination for having left it.

This matters more than it might initially seem. The weight of self-recrimination after reversion is not a neutral tax on the experience. It is itself a pressure that makes the next reversion more likely, because it reactivates the very organization the reframe was working to shift: the one that treats the self as a mechanism that failed and needs to be corrected through force. To recognize reversion as structural rather than personal is to remove that additional weight: to return to the new orientation without the overhead of having first established that you are the problem.

•••

When the frame fits, when the position is accurate, when effort is located at the level where it can reach, movement feels like itself.

This is difficult to describe without sounding either mystical or like the setup for a productivity metaphor, so let's be specific about what it means. Movement that feels like itself is not effortless. It is not free of the ordinary friction that any sustained engagement with something real involves. It is not characterized by the absence of difficulty.

What it is characterized by is the absence of the specific kind of resistance that comes from working against your own system's organization. The direction is not being forced against the grain of what the system can sustain. The commitment fits the actual structure rather than requiring it to pretend to an organization it doesn't have. The effort is located where it can connect with what is actually happening rather than being absorbed into the overhead of self-coercion.

The result is that things happen. Not magically: you are still doing the work, still spending the energy, still navigating the actual difficulty of the actual situation. But the progress is proportionate to the effort in a way that was not true before. The investment lands somewhere. The engagement accumulates rather than evaporating into the gap between what the system is organized around and what the effort was aimed at.

There is also a quality of direction clarity that comes with this. Not certainty about outcomes (self-organizing systems navigating actual complexity do not produce outcome certainty, and any account that promises otherwise is selling something the field deliberately does not sell). But clarity about direction: a sense of what the situation actually requires that is distinguishable from what urgency or habit or the current frame's organization says it requires. When you are standing somewhere that makes the next move visible, the next move tends to be visible. You do not need to construct it from abstract principles or force it from an arbitrary decision. It is there because the position makes it accessible.

This is what this book has been pointing toward throughout. Not a specific outcome. Not a set of achievements that verify that the reframe worked. A different quality of engagement with whatever is being navigated: effort that is proportionate, stuck that is readable, commitment that is sustainable because it fits the actual system rather than overriding it, movement that accumulates because it is aimed at the right level. These qualities are available. They have always been available. What changes is the position from which you can access them.

• • •

This book does not end with instructions.

You have a structural account of why effort fails. Not as a metaphor or a motivational reframe: as an account of what is actually happening when hard work doesn't produce movement. You have a working model of yourself as a self-organizing system that reorganizes through meaning rather than through force. You have language for the difference between effort applied at the right level and effort applied at the wrong one. You have a reframe for stuck, for paralysis, for the insight that fades, for the change that doesn't hold.

What you do with this is yours. The book doesn't prescribe next steps because action that follows from accurate orientation doesn't need to be directed. You know what question to ask when things aren't working. You know what it means to attend to position before performance. You know that the system's resistance is information, not defiance. You know that reversion is structural rather than personal. These things, once understood, change what is visible, and what is visible determines what is available, more reliably than any technique applied from a position that can't see clearly where it's aimed.

For those who want to go further, the Collected Founding Papers of Applied Philosophy of Human Systems are available. The companion monograph (included as Appendix A) maps their full architecture: the field's working assumptions, its vocabulary, the structure of all three volumes of the founding papers, and the five domains the field illuminates. These are invitations, not requirements. They exist for readers who want the complete structural picture behind the ideas encountered here. This book is complete without them.

What the work itself asks is only this: that its observations be tested in experience, and kept or set aside based on whether they clarify. Not loyalty. Not adoption. Not continued engagement. Just honest testing. The field has no interest in adherence. It has an interest in being useful, and usefulness is determined by whether contact with these ideas changes what you can see and what you can do about it.

Effort fails when it is applied at the wrong level. That is the complete answer this book set out to deliver. And the complete answer changes something, not because it provides a new plan, but because it locates the problem accurately. Once the problem is located accurately, it belongs to you in a way it did not before. You know where you are standing. You know what level the work lives at. You know what question to ask.

Appendix

The ideas in this book did not originate here. They come from a larger field called Applied Philosophy of Human Systems (APHS), and the book you just read represents one application of that field's observations: focused, practical, and deliberately stripped of the field's full architecture in favor of its most immediate utility. If the argument landed, you have already been working inside APHS without the formal introduction.

This monograph provides that introduction. It was written to orient readers before they enter the Collected Founding Papers of APHS, a three-volume set of twenty-one papers that establishes the field in full. Its structure maps four dimensions of the field simultaneously: the working assumptions behind its observations, the vocabulary it uses with specific precision, the domains of human experience it addresses, and the arc of the three volumes through which it was articulated. Some of what it covers will be familiar from what you have already read. Encountering that material here, in its structural form rather than in application, tends to land differently. What felt like a practical reframe often reveals itself as one expression of something with considerably more reach. The monograph is an invitation to see the whole picture. It is not a requirement for anything.

APPLIED PHILOSOPHY OF HUMAN SYSTEMS™

Monograph Series · Orientation

Monograph ORI-01

A Reader's Orientation to Applied Philosophy of Human Systems

---

James Zboran

2026

aphsfield.com

Abstract

Applied Philosophy of Human Systems™ (APHS™) is a field of inquiry concerned with how human beings function as self-organizing systems within lived contexts. It occupies the gap between philosophy that remains abstract and applied domains that default to technique. It changes what becomes visible without prescribing what to do with what you see.

A complete grasp of the field requires engaging four distinct dimensions simultaneously: its assumptions (what the field takes to be true about how human systems work); its vocabulary (terms tuned to carry precise meanings that differ from everyday usage); its domains (the areas of human experience the field directs its attention toward); and its arc (the three-volume structure through which the field was articulated), a structure that enacts the very process it describes.

This monograph maps all four in full. It is not a summary of the field's content. It is an orientation to the field's architecture: the terrain a reader will encounter when they enter the Collected Founding Papers. Its function is to provide enough structural clarity that when the founding papers are engaged directly, they land with more precision rather than less.

Nothing in this monograph requires adoption. Each distinction can be tested in lived experience and set aside without consequence if it does not clarify. The field does not depend on agreement, allegiance, or continued engagement. Its coherence lies in what it describes, not in whether anyone finds those descriptions useful.

•••

Section Map

• • •

0. Orientation

This monograph exists because of a gap, not in the field itself but in how it is encountered.

The Collected Founding Papers of Applied Philosophy of Human Systems are precise, carefully structured, and complete on their own terms. They establish what the field observes, how it operates, where it stops, and why. For a reader who comes to them with no prior orientation, they are navigable. For a reader who arrives with a clear sense of the field's architecture (its assumptions, vocabulary, domains, and arc), they land differently. More precisely. With less interpretive noise and more structural clarity.

This monograph provides that prior orientation. It does not replace the founding papers. It is a map of the territory they occupy, offered to a reader before they enter.

A note on what this is not: it is not an introduction in the sense of a simplified or popularized account. The distinctions here are the same ones operative in the founding papers, presented in their structural relationships rather than unfolded at full depth. Readers who want depth will find it in the papers themselves. What this monograph provides is breadth: the shape of the whole before its parts are engaged.

A note on how to read it: this is not material to be retained and applied. It is an orienting pass through terrain that will be traversed again, more slowly, in the founding papers. Read it as you would read a map before a journey: not to memorize every feature, but to carry a sense of the whole into the territory.

. . .

1. The Assumptions

APHS operates from a layered set of working assumptions, not axioms offered for universal acceptance, but patterns that appear consistently when human experience is observed over time in real contexts. Their value lies not in theoretical elegance but in whether they clarify what is already happening and reduce unnecessary friction in interpretation and action. They are organized across six categories, each operating at a different level of the field's architecture.

A note on how to read these: they are not a checklist to accept or reject before engaging the field. They are the ground the field stands on, made visible so that when a reader encounters an observation that seems to contradict their assumptions about how people work, they have a place to locate the disagreement. Engaging a working assumption critically is one of the most productive things a reader can do with it.

Category 1: Core Assumptions (What Human Systems Are)

Five assumptions constitute the field's foundational description of the human being as a system rather than a mechanism. They form the ground on which everything else stands, and they are mutually reinforcing: each one makes the others more intelligible.

Human systems self-organize: change unfolds within them, not on them. Thoughts, emotions, behaviors, identities, and meanings are not independent components to be managed in isolation. They emerge from ongoing interaction between the individual and their environment. Change is not something done to a system. It is something that unfolds within it when conditions shift. Stability and movement are properties of organization, not moral achievements or failures. Attempts to impose order through force (whether through discipline, technique, or coercive frameworks) tend to generate resistance or instability precisely because they ignore how organization naturally arises. The system is not defying the intervention. It is responding accurately to pressure it cannot integrate.

Human systems are meaning-driven: they respond to interpretation, not just force. The same pressure applied to a human system can produce completely different results depending on how it is interpreted. A demand for faster output might land as threat, invalidation, or opportunity, depending on context. This makes force unreliable as a change mechanism. It is not the magnitude of pressure that determines the response. It is what that pressure means within the system's current organization. This is why two people in identical circumstances can move in opposite directions, and why technique applied without attention to meaning so often produces compliance without engagement.

Agency is emergent, not fixed. Within APHS, agency is not a capacity strengthened through willpower or instruction. It increases or decreases depending on how coherently someone is oriented within their actual circumstances. When interpretation aligns with real constraints and signals, choices become clearer and action follows naturally. When interpretation is distorted, agency contracts, regardless of effort. A lack of movement often indicates that the system is responding accurately to a misaligned frame. Restoring agency is less about motivation and more about reorientation. This reframes many familiar struggles: stuck is not the same as lazy, paralysis is not the same as avoidance, and protective inaction is not the same as failure of will.

Meaning is participatory: it arises through engagement, not prescription. Meaning is neither discovered as a fixed truth waiting to be found, nor constructed arbitrarily through personal preference. It arises through participation: shaped by context, relationship, history, and consequence. What matters to a person cannot be abstracted from where they are standing, what they are responsible for, or what they are navigating. This assumption resists both relativism and universalism. Meaning is not purely subjective, but neither can it be handed to someone from outside. Attempts to prescribe meaning interrupt the participatory process through which meaning actually forms, which is why meaning imposed from outside rarely holds, regardless of its quality.

Coherence is sought through interaction, not control. Internal alignment and stability emerge when interpretations, emotions, and actions are allowed to respond to one another honestly within real constraints. When control replaces that interaction (when parts of the system are suppressed, overridden, or forced into uniformity) systems may appear orderly on the surface while becoming brittle underneath. Coherence is not agreement, consistency, or calm. A system under genuine tension can be coherent. A system that appears orderly on the surface can lack it entirely. Coherence is what makes effort productive rather than exhausting, and its presence or absence determines which options are genuinely available rather than merely visible.

These five assumptions are mutually reinforcing. Coherence is why systems resist force: they are protecting their own organization. Agency expands when orientation is coherent because the system is aligned with actual conditions. Meaning cannot be prescribed because imposed meaning disrupts rather than creates coherence. Together they point in one direction: a human system cannot be managed the way a machine can. The levers are different, and applying the wrong ones does not just fail; it typically makes things worse.

Category 2: Operating Assumptions (How APHS Observes)

These assumptions describe how the field itself stands in relation to what it observes: its methodological posture and epistemic commitments. They are not claims about human systems; they are claims about how APHS attends to them.

The observer is inside the system, not outside it. Observation within APHS is participatory. The observer is not positioned outside experience attempting neutrality or detachment. They are inside lived experience, aware that interpretation shapes what is seen. This resists false objectivity without collapsing into subjectivism. What matters is not whether an observation is detached but whether it remains honest, repeatable in experience, and responsive to contradiction. An observation that holds across varied contexts and survives contact with real decision-making, responsibility, and uncertainty is treated as more reliable than one that resolves neatly in theory.

Uncertainty is a condition of adaptation, not a problem to eliminate. Human systems are embedded in environments that change, resist prediction, and generate novel conditions. Attempts to reduce uncertainty through rigid models or premature certainty tend to increase fragility rather than resilience. APHS maintains conceptual openness: its distinctions are held lightly and always subject to revision when contexts shift or patterns fail to hold. This does not weaken the field. It preserves the capacity to remain responsive to what is actually happening rather than defending what was previously concluded.

Models are judged by whether they work, not whether they are metaphysically true. APHS does not claim its models are ultimate accounts of reality. It claims they are useful orientations that can be tested in lived experience. A model that generates accurate patterns, restores navigational clarity, and enables movement is a functional model, regardless of whether it describes the ultimate nature of what it represents. If it works, it serves. If it does not, it can be discarded without consequence. This is not relativism. It is accurate scoping about the level at which the field operates.

Orientation is privileged over solutions. Solutions imply closure: a problem defined, an intervention applied, an outcome achieved. Orientation remains ongoing. It supports navigation rather than arrival, responsiveness rather than control. This prevents the field from collapsing into a system of answers that must be defended. By resisting the pressure to resolve, APHS avoids the failure mode of fields that become rigid around their own conclusions. It remains a domain of inquiry that supports clarity, coherence, and movement precisely because it does not insist on certainty, compliance, or completion.

Long-horizon patterns across varied contexts matter more than phenomena isolated under controlled conditions. Many aspects of human experience (meaning, agency, identity, coherence) do not reveal themselves cleanly under reduction. They emerge over time, across varied conditions, in the friction between intention and circumstance. APHS privileges what persists across that variation over what can be measured in controlled settings. This is not anti-empirical. It is accurate scoping about where the relevant patterns actually live.

Category 3: Structural Assumptions (How the Field Holds Itself)

These assumptions describe the field's relationship to those who engage it and to its own authority and scope. They are less about what APHS observes and more about what it claims, and deliberately does not claim, for itself.

The field owns nothing. APHS assumes no authority over how its observations are used, applied, or extended. It does not certify practitioners, approve applications, or claim lineage over downstream work. No allegiance, attribution, or fidelity is required. Coherence in the field arises through shared orientation, not enforced consistency. This non-ownership posture carries ethical weight: by refusing to claim authority over application, the field preserves participant autonomy. No one is positioned as an expert over another's experience, and no interpretation obligates action. This also protects the field from becoming extractive, requiring loyalty, identity adoption, or belief in order to function.

Participation requires no adoption, allegiance, or belief. Engaging APHS does not mean taking on a worldview, joining something, or committing to continued engagement. A distinction can be tried, inhabited provisionally, and discarded without consequence. The field makes no demands and tracks no progress. Its observations stand or fall based on whether they clarify, not on whether the reader is committed to them.

The field is living, not complete. APHS treats itself as a starting point rather than a terminus. New distinctions may emerge, existing ones may deepen, and blind spots may become visible as others test the field's observations across varied contexts. It grows not by accumulation of content but by continued attention to how human systems actually organize themselves. A completed body of knowledge cannot evolve. A living field remains responsive.

Responsibility belongs to participation, not outcomes. A person engaging APHS is accountable for how clearly they stand and how honestly they participate, not for what the system then does. Outcomes depend on factors no single person controls. This relocation of responsibility is not a reduction of it. It is a more accurate placement: applied to where a person actually has influence, rather than to results that depend on the responses of systems operating by their own coherence requirements.

Influence and authority are different things. APHS can inform without authorizing, clarify without controlling, and shape without owning. A framework informed by the field is informed by it: not an APHS method, not an APHS-approved approach. The designer remains accountable for their own work. The user remains free to evaluate applications on their own merits. The field benefits when its observations prove useful but does not depend on that usefulness for coherence. This three-way independence (between field, designer, and end-user) prevents the ideological capture that occurs when fields attempt to control their applications, and prevents the field from becoming a brand requiring protection rather than an inquiry remaining open.

Category 4: Phenomenological Assumptions (How Experience and Change Actually Work)

These assumptions describe specific dynamics of human experience that APHS treats as observable features of how systems behave: not theories, but patterns that recur reliably when attention is sustained across varied conditions and contexts.

Frame shifts cannot be forced: they are recognized, not executed. Conscious awareness does not produce frame shifts through intention or effort. It notices when they have already occurred. The shift is an event within the system, emerging when conditions destabilize the existing frame sufficiently. This means frame shifting cannot be pursued as a goal. Attempting to force a frame shift (through willpower, deliberate reframing, or technique) tends to reinforce the existing frame by treating it as the stable ground from which the effort is being made. What allows frames to shift is not decision but conditions: lived contradiction where behavior and frame misalign repeatedly, exposure to alternative structures that organize meaning more coherently, or gradual erosion of the frame's stability as accumulated incoherence weakens it.

Explanation follows reorganization: it does not cause it. Language arrives after a shift, describing what has already changed rather than producing the change through articulation. Insight is perceptual before it is verbal. The reorganization precedes the account of it. This means people often act from a new frame before they can fully describe it, which is appropriate. The attempt to achieve full verbal clarity before moving inverts the actual sequence. It assumes that understanding must precede action when in fact action often clarifies understanding. Expecting complete articulation before allowing movement is a reliable way to stall reorganization.

Most reorganization occurs at other-than-conscious levels. The conscious mind is a participant in the system, not its commander. Frames are maintained and reorganized at levels largely outside conscious control, through emotional weighting, somatic patterning, and meaning structures that operate automatically. This is why conscious willpower is such an unreliable change mechanism: it cannot reach where the actual work is happening. Recognizing this removes pressure without removing agency. People do not need to think their way into different frames. They need to recognize what frame is currently operating and whether it still fits.

Struggle is often structural, not personal. When effort consistently fails to produce movement, the issue is usually positional rather than a reflection of character, capacity, or motivation. The person is standing in a location from which the movement they are attempting is not available: not because they are insufficiently committed, disciplined, or capable, but because the position itself forecloses the movement. The question shifts from *what is wrong with me?* to *where am I standing?* That shift is not rhetorical. It relocates the problem from character to structure, which is almost always more addressable.

Position precedes improvement. Optimization is only useful once direction is sound. Someone can improve steadily while feeling worse, achieve more while mattering less, become more capable while growing less satisfied, if they are optimizing in the wrong direction. Standing clearly comes before improving performance. This is not about abandoning discipline or effort. It is about ensuring that effort is directed by accurate orientation rather than by momentum within a frame that no longer fits.

Optimization applied to misalignment produces refined misalignment.

Category 5: Mind Assumptions (What Kind of System Consciousness Is)

The books articulate a working model of consciousness adjacent to the field, not foundational to it but available to those who want a coherent account of why APHS observations hold. APHS functions without this model; the field stands on its observations rather than on the theory. What the model provides is intelligibility: it makes certain patterns comprehensible that would otherwise seem paradoxical, particularly for readers whose prior assumptions position consciousness as the executive center that decides and controls.

Mind operates across multiple concurrent modes of awareness, none hierarchically superior. These include conscious awareness (logic, language, deliberate attention, narrative construction), subconscious patterning (habitual responses, emotional associations, automatic interpretations), unconscious and somatic intelligence (bodily signals, deep pattern recognition, instinctual response), collective and archetypal structures (culturally inherited frames, shared meaning patterns, narrative archetypes), and observer-level awareness (the capacity to notice one's own mental processes, to see a frame rather than only through it). All are active simultaneously, each contributing specialized intelligence.

Conscious awareness is a participant and interface, not an executive. It handles logic, language, deliberate attention, and narrative construction, and it provides orientation. But it does not command reorganization. When someone attempts to manage their own frame-level change through conscious control, they are applying a tool suited to one function to a task that operates at a level beyond its reach. The strength of conscious awareness lies in interface and coordination: setting direction, naming contradictions, choosing where to direct attention. These are real contributions. They shape how the rest of the system organizes itself. But they do not override the distributed intelligence that maintains coherence.

Frames are maintained at other-than-conscious levels. A frame does not dissolve because it has been recognized as inadequate. It continues activating through emotional weighting, somatic patterning, and meaning structures, which is why conscious recognition of a frame's inadequacy does not immediately dissolve it. The person can explain the new perspective convincingly while continuing to operate from the old frame. This is not hypocrisy or lack of commitment. It is the system functioning as designed: patterns maintained at other-than-conscious levels continue until the conditions maintaining them shift, regardless of what conscious awareness has concluded.

The system cannot be commanded from the top down. Attempting to centralize all function within conscious control interrupts the distributed intelligence that maintains coherence. The system resists not because it is broken but because it is functioning as designed: protecting the coordination that keeps it integrated. This is why force applied inward (self-coercion, suppression, overriding of signals) produces compliance that is unstable and costly. Once the force is removed, the system reasserts patterns that reflect its actual organization.

Stillness and reduced effort often precede insight, not the reverse. Conscious awareness registers the shift once reorganization has reached a threshold of coherence, after it has already been proceeding outside awareness. The suddenness of insight is real from the perspective of narration; the underlying process was incremental. The implication is that the interval that feels like nothing happening may be the interval during which the most consequential work is occurring. Attempts to force movement during that interval interrupt rather than accelerate it. APHS holds this as an adjacent model, not a foundational one. The field functions without it.

Category 6: Change Assumptions (What Kinds of Change Exist and What They Require)

One of APHS's most practically consequential contributions is a hard distinction between two fundamentally different kinds of change that most frameworks, methods, and systems of personal development conflate. Confusing them creates the characteristic failure mode of applied domains: applying the right tool to the wrong kind of problem, intensifying exhaustion without producing movement, and interpreting the absence of results as evidence that more effort is required.

Translational change moves within a stable frame through effort, strategy, and adjustment. The coordinates within which progress is defined remain constant. A person working toward a goal, improving a skill, building a relationship, or developing a practice is engaged in translational change. It produces reliable results when the frame organizing perception is accurate. It responds to effort, discipline, and incremental adjustment. Its limits appear not from insufficient effort but from the fact that it operates within structures it cannot reorganize.

Transformational change reorganizes the frame itself. It is a structural shift in the coordinates from which perception, meaning, and available options are organized. After a frame shift, what was previously invisible becomes apparent, what seemed necessary becomes optional, and what appeared impossible reveals itself as available. Transformational change is non-linear, often irreversible, and cannot be forced or scheduled. It occurs when systemic conditions align in ways that allow frame reorganization: when lived contradiction between behavior and frame accumulates sufficiently, when exposure to an alternative structure that organizes meaning more coherently creates an available shift, or when the frame's stability erodes as its incoherence becomes undeniable.

Applying translational effort during transformation anchors the old frame in place. This is the crucial failure mode the distinction is designed to prevent. Increased effort, redoubled discipline, refined strategy: all of these operate from within the frame that is attempting to shift. They take the existing frame as given and optimize within it. In doing so, they reinforce precisely the structural patterns that need to reorganize. The system invests more deeply in the frame's stability at the moment when that stability most needs to loosen.

The appropriate response to transformation is orientation, not action. During transformation, clarity about what is reorganizing is itself the change, occurring at the level where frames organize experience. The instinct to do something with the recognition (to apply it, convert it into technique, build a practice from it) is understandable and also the move most likely to interrupt the reorganization before it completes.

What looks like stagnation from outside may be profound reorganization from within. Contemporary systems of evaluation are calibrated to detect translational progress: movement toward measurable goals, incremental improvements in performance, visible changes in behavior. They cannot detect structural reorganization happening at a level below behavior. Someone in the middle of frame-level transformation may appear, from the outside, to be stuck, stagnant, or going backwards. From the inside, they may be in the most consequential interval of change they have ever experienced. The instruments are wrong for the process they are trying to read.

...

2. The Vocabulary

The books explicitly describe their key terms as tuned rather than simply defined: positioned so that what follows reads as intended. Each carries precise meaning that differs from everyday usage, and misreading even one of them is among the most common ways engagement with the field goes wrong. The vocabulary builds across the three books: Book I introduces the core architecture, Book II extends it into application, and Book III refines the reader's relationship to concepts already active rather than adding independent structure.

A note before the terms: these definitions resist the usual firmness. That resistance is not a failure of precision. It reflects the character of the field they serve. Each term is an orienting frame, not a fixed container. The definitions that follow are designed to be inhabited and tested rather than memorized.

Book I: The Core Architecture

Human system. A person, group, or organization understood as a self-organizing system rather than a mechanism. The key word is *understood*: this is a working frame for observation, not an ontological claim about what people ultimately are. Human systems do not respond predictably to force the way machines do. They reorganize through meaning, coherence, and context. Using this frame shifts the questions available: not *what is wrong with this person and how do we fix it*, but *how is this system organized and what does it need in order to move.*

Frame. An orientational structure that organizes meaning, emotional weighting, and perceived options before conscious interpretation occurs. Frames are not beliefs or opinions. They operate below deliberate thought, filtering what seems relevant, possible, or necessary. They are rarely experienced as thoughts because they are not thoughts. They are the structures within which thoughts occur: the patterns that determine what thinking is about and the contexts that give thoughts their meaning. A frame shift is not a decision. It is a reorganization that arrives before the language to describe it does.

Orientation. The structure from which perception and response arise: where someone is standing in relation to their circumstances. Orientation is prior to attitude, intention, or perspective. It is not chosen deliberately; it shapes what choices appear available. Restoring orientation means something more foundational than changing one's outlook: it addresses the position from which the outlook is generated. When orientation shifts, what becomes possible shifts with it. Two people standing in genuinely different orientations toward the same circumstances are not in disagreement about interpretations. They are operating from different grounds.

Coherence. The dynamic alignment within a system that allows movement to occur without force. Critically: coherence is not agreement, consistency, or calm. A system under genuine tension can be coherent. A system that appears orderly on the surface can lack it. Coherence is what makes effort productive rather than exhausting: the condition under which the system can move without working against itself. Its presence or absence determines which options are genuinely available rather than merely visible. Incoherence is not a moral failure. It is a structural state that contracts the range of sustainable choices until conditions restore alignment.

Force. Pressure applied in a way the system cannot integrate without contradicting its own organization. Force is not the same as effort. Effort is energy expenditure; it may or may not be well-placed. Force specifically names the misapplication of pressure: pressure the system is organized to resist. Resistance to force is not defiance or weakness. It is self-protection: the system maintaining its integrity against an input that would require it to reorganize in a way that contradicts its current coherence. When force is met with resistance, the appropriate response is not more force. It is a different kind of engagement.

Agency. Not willpower, capability, or discipline. Agency in APHS is emergent: it expands when orientation is coherent with actual conditions, and contracts when it is not. A lack of movement is often a positioning problem, not a capacity problem. Agency is also participatory; it operates through clear positioning and coherent presence rather than through command or control. Someone with contracted agency is not someone who lacks strength. They are someone whose current orientation does not make movement available. Restoring agency begins with restoring orientation, not with applying more determination.

Field. A domain of sustained observation and clarification: not a method, system, or framework. A field changes what you can see. It does not prescribe what to do with what you see. APHS is explicitly a field in this sense. The distinction matters: when a field is mistaken for a method, the orientation it provides is lost beneath the techniques it is expected to supply. A field that becomes a method ceases to function as a field. It becomes one more thing competing with other methods at the level where the field's actual contribution (the change in what becomes visible) was operating.

Functional model. A model evaluated by whether it works (whether it generates accurate patterns, restores navigational clarity, and enables movement) rather than by whether it is metaphysically true. APHS does not claim its models are ultimate accounts of reality. It claims they are useful orientations that can be tested in lived experience and discarded without consequence if they do not serve. This is not relativism. A functional model can be rigorous, testable, and reliable. The criterion of evaluation is simply different: does it clarify what is already happening, rather than does it correspond to an ultimate account of reality.

Book II: Extensions into Application

Integration. The process through which a frame shift propagates across the interconnected patterns of a system. Integration is not reflection, emotional processing, or the work of deliberately absorbing insight. It is what a self-organizing system does when left to its own timing after reorientation occurs. The system reorganizes its habitual responses, emotional associations, and behavioral patterns to align with the new frame, not through conscious direction but through the ongoing adjustment that self-organization naturally performs. Forcing movement before integration completes does not accelerate the process. It strains it, often reinstating the very patterns the frame shift disrupted.

Optimization. Refining performance within an existing frame: improving execution, reducing inefficiency, increasing output along a stable set of coordinates. Optimization is legitimate and often productive, but it addresses only problems that exist within a frame that already fits. When the frame itself is misaligned, optimization makes a poorly positioned system perform better while remaining poorly positioned. The masking effect is significant: a system that is visibly improving along measurable dimensions can become increasingly committed to a direction that does not serve it. Optimization obscures orientation errors rather than correcting them.

Translational change. Movement within a stable frame through effort, strategy, and adjustment. Produces reliable results when the frame organizing perception is accurate. Responds to discipline, technique, and incremental refinement. Its limits appear when the frame itself no longer fits, at which point translational effort intensifies exhaustion rather than producing movement. Translational change is not lesser than transformational change. It is appropriate to its conditions. The problem arises only when it is applied to conditions that require something different.

Transformational change. Reorganization of the frame itself: a structural shift in the coordinates from which perception, meaning, and available options are organized. During transformation, familiar markers of progress disappear because those markers were defined within the frame that is shifting. This instability is a necessary feature of the process, not evidence of failure. Transformational change cannot be forced, scheduled, or managed into completion. It can be supported by conditions that allow the existing frame's instability to register, by reducing the pressure that reinforces the old frame, and by maintaining orientation through the interval of reorganization.

Participation. The form agency takes in self-organizing systems. Not passivity, and not command. Influence operates through positioning and attunement rather than force or direction. Someone who participates coherently, standing clearly, responding to what is actually happening rather than to what they wish were happening, and maintaining their orientation under pressure without imposing it on others, shapes the systems they move through without controlling them. Leadership as an expression of participation means standing clearly enough that others can orient themselves relative to your clarity, not compelling them to follow.

Protective choosing. The system's accurate response when all visible options would cause more damage than remaining uncommitted. Not avoidance, indecision, or failure of will, but a genuine structural condition. The word *accurate* matters: protective choosing describes what a coherent system does when the frame does not yet contain a sustainable path forward. Forcing commitment when protective choosing is operative does not resolve the structural condition. It produces a commitment the system cannot sustain, which either collapses or requires continuous effort to maintain, consuming energy that could otherwise address the conditions preventing resourceful alternatives.

Resourceful options. Alternatives the system can actually sustain without continuous effort to maintain them. Distinguished from forced commitments: choices that appear available but require the system to work against its own organization to hold them. Coherence, orientation, and reduced pressure expand the range of resourceful options. Incoherence, disorientation, and urgency contract it. When orientation is clear, the sustainable choice often feels obvious rather than deliberated, not because the choice is easy, but because it aligns with how the system is actually organized. What made this possible is not improved decision-making skill. It is clearer orientation.

Book III: Refinements for Integration

Systemization. The conversion of orientation into repeatable method: extracting principles, building checklists, creating frameworks from what has been encountered. Systemization is not wrong in general. In many domains it is exactly what makes insight useful. But this work functions differently: it operates through perceptual reorganization, not through procedures to apply. When orientation is converted into system, what worked by changing how things are seen becomes something that can be executed without seeing anything new. The capacity for ongoing navigation is replaced by the appearance of completed understanding. The mechanism that made the orientation valuable is precisely what systemization eliminates.

Open frame. An orientational structure that can still move, responsive to new experience rather than fixed into final form. An open frame is not an unfinished one. It is not ambiguous, provisional, or waiting for its conclusions to arrive. It is complete in the sense that it organizes perception accurately; it remains open in the sense that it continues adapting to what it encounters. Closure converts this responsiveness into memory: what adjusted to experience becomes interpretation to be recalled. Leaving the frame open is not a discipline to practice. It is a condition to recognize and avoid disrupting. What the reader is being asked to leave open at the end of the arc is not unfinished. It is complete in a sense that requires remaining open.

Reading for alignment. The mode of engagement the work asks of the reader: inhabiting a vantage point rather than extracting tools or harvesting principles. Reading for alignment is not passive. It involves genuine attention to whether the distinctions encountered are reorganizing perception. But the test is not whether principles can be recalled and explained. It is whether navigation has changed: whether things previously invisible are now visible, whether options previously hidden are now apparent. Readers who approach the material looking for content to possess will miss what it offers. The value is in perceptual reorganization, not in the possession of information.

Holding without gripping. Remaining available to a new frame during the period when it is present but not yet stable. Holding is not vigilance and not enforcement. Vigilance tries to protect the new frame from loss; enforcement tries to use it as a rule. Both convert the frame into an object to be managed rather than a reorganization to be inhabited. Gripping stops the process it means to preserve. What is actually required during instability is availability: a willingness to see through the new frame when it is accessible without requiring it to be dominant when it is not.

Reversion. Return to previous patterns under pressure from embedded systems (relationships, roles, environments) organized around the previous frame. Reversion is a structural response, not evidence of frame inaccuracy. When a person reorganizes and the social systems they are embedded in have not, those systems continue operating as if the previous frame is intact. The pressure this creates (through expectation, obligation, and familiar emotional cues) can trigger reversion without any decision to return. Reversion is not failure. It is the embedded system pushing back. Recognizing reversion as structural constraint rather than personal failure keeps integration intact.

Invisible integration. Reorganization that proceeds without conscious tracking, visible feedback, or behavioral announcement. Most deep integration is invisible while it is occurring. Perception shifts at scales too fine to observe. Habitual responses adjust incrementally. The system reorganizes at levels below the threshold of conscious awareness. The common misreading converts this invisible interval into stagnation, concluding that because nothing visible is happening, nothing is happening. The appropriate response to invisible integration is to stop attempting to force visible movement, not because nothing matters, but because the process is proceeding correctly at a level where interference disrupts rather than accelerates it.

Closure. The conversion of living orientation into completed, fixed understanding. Closure makes the work easier to summarize and harder to use. When a frame is closed, it can be carried and explained; what it cannot do is continue adapting to what the reader encounters. Book III treats closure not as a failure of discipline but as a structural change with predictable consequences: ongoing perceptual reorganization is replaced by the possession of finished understanding. The work that follows does not provide closure, not because something is missing, but because closure would eliminate the condition under which the work continues to function.

· · ·

3. The Domains

APHS illuminates five named domains of human experience and organization. These are not isolated topics. They are interrelated expressions of the same underlying systemic dynamics: each one is a different angle on how meaning-based, self-organizing systems actually function. In each domain, the field looks upstream: rather than addressing behavior directly, it asks how effort becomes misapplied, how coherence is lost, how motivation erodes, and what restores the conditions under which movement resumes. Understanding any one domain fully requires the others; they are facets of the same territory, not separate territories.

Agency

How choice expands or contracts depending on interpretation rather than effort. Agency is an emergent property of coherent orientation rather than a fixed capacity. When interpretation aligns with actual constraints and possibilities, choices become clear and action follows naturally. When it is distorted, agency contracts, not because willpower is insufficient but because the system is responding accurately to misaligned framing.

This reframe changes almost everything about how struggle is interpreted. Stuck is not the same as weak. Paralysis is not the same as avoidance. Protective choosing is not the same as failure. In each case, APHS asks the prior question: where is the system standing, and does that position allow movement? When a person who has been working harder and harder without results discovers that the problem is positional rather than personal (that they have been standing somewhere from which the movement they are attempting is not available), the relief is often immediate. Not because anything external has changed, but because the frame through which the situation was being organized has shifted.

Agency also reveals itself as participatory in character: influence operates through clear standing and coherent positioning rather than through control over outcomes. This connects directly to the leadership domain; the two illuminate each other.

Leadership

How coherence and trust emerge without reliance on force or control. Leadership organized around authority and command produces compliance without engagement, order without capacity, systems that function while their leader is present and collapse when they leave. In APHS terms, command-based leadership is an attempt to manage meaning-based systems through mechanical means: the levers are wrong, and the results reflect that mismatch.

APHS observes a different form of leadership: emergent rather than appointed. Someone stands clearly in relation to what matters. They maintain that position consistently under pressure.

They respond to challenges without losing coherence. Others notice and begin to orient themselves relative to that clarity. The person has become a reference point not through command but through the reliability of their positioning.

This form of leadership preserves agency in others rather than suppressing it. When someone leads through coherent participation, others remain free to orient themselves differently: to align, diverge, or build on what is offered. Their participation is more engaged and more adaptive than it would be under command, precisely because it was never coerced. The connection to the agency domain is direct: leadership that preserves agency expands the coherence of the systems it touches; leadership that suppresses agency contracts it.

Time

How past, present, and future are organized through meaning rather than chronology alone. Time in APHS is a domain of meaning organized by frames, not simply a sequence of moments. The same history can feel like evidence of failure in one frame and evidence of resilience in another. The same future can feel foreclosed or available depending on what the current frame makes visible as possible.

Temporal disorientation (feeling stuck in the past, unable to imagine a future, disconnected from continuity) is, in APHS terms, a frame problem rather than a time problem. What is experienced as being trapped in history is often the interpretive structure through which the timeline is being organized. When that structure reorganizes, temporal experience reorganizes with it. The past does not change. The meaning it carries does.

This domain is the territory most directly addressed by downstream applications such as Timeline Surfing™, which translates APHS observations about time, identity, and continuity into navigable practices. APHS itself does not provide those practices. It describes the dynamics they work with, at a level of abstraction that remains prior to any specific application.

Identity

How self-concept stabilizes as a residue of action and context rather than as a fixed cause. Identity in APHS is not a core self that precedes experience and expresses itself through behavior. It is what has organized itself through how a person has stood, acted, and interpreted experience over time: a pattern that stabilizes, functions as ground, and reorganizes when frames reorganize.

When frames shift, identity shifts correspondingly. This is why transformation can feel so destabilizing: the person may recognize that self-concepts held firmly no longer feel accurate, that ways of being that felt essential have become optional, that aspects of self previously suppressed or invisible have emerged. The transformation affects not only how the person sees but who they understand themselves to be. This is not a pathological condition. It is the normal experience of frame-level reorganization in the domain of identity.

Identity is also, for this reason, addressable. If it is residue rather than fixed essence, it is shaped by the conditions within which a person stands and acts. Changing the frame changes what identity can organize around. This does not mean identity is unstable or arbitrary; it typically has considerable continuity and coherence. It means that identity, like frames, can reorganize when conditions support it, and that attempting to hold identity fixed during transformation is one of the most reliable ways to interrupt the reorganization that is trying to occur.

Systems

How human systems adapt, resist, or reorganize in response to pressure and feedback. This is the overarching domain that ties all the others together. Every phenomenon APHS addresses (agency, leadership, time, identity) is an expression of how meaning-based, self-organizing systems function. The systems domain attends to these dynamics at the level of groups, organizations, and relationships as well as individuals, since the same patterns appear across all scales.

Human systems share structural properties: they self-organize, they respond to meaning rather than force, they resist what they cannot integrate, and they reorganize when conditions shift sufficiently. Understanding these properties changes how pressure is applied, how change is approached, and how leadership is exercised, across contexts from the personal to the organizational. A group that cannot move is often in the same positional predicament as an individual who cannot move: not lacking capability, but standing somewhere from which the movement being attempted is not available.

The systems domain is where APHS is most useful for those who design frameworks, methods, and practices for others. Knowing how human systems actually organize themselves (what they respond to, what they resist, what they require in order to reorganize): this is the upstream understanding that makes application-level work coherent rather than arbitrary. Applications built without this understanding tend to apply the right tool to the wrong level, producing visible results that mask the structural dynamics they were meant to address.

• • •

4. The Arc

The three books of the Collected Founding Papers form a single movement. Their division is not arbitrary: each addresses a genuinely distinct phase of engagement with how human systems change. Together they enact the process APHS describes. The structure is not packaging for content; it is itself an expression of the field's understanding.

Three observations from the field correspond directly to the three books. You cannot reorganize from within a frame you cannot see: this is Book I's territory. Reorganization cannot be forced but can be supported: this is Book II's. Integration proceeds in its own timing and collapses when managed: this is Book III's. The arc as a whole is a description of how transformation actually unfolds, and a demonstration of what it looks like when the structure of a work respects the process it describes.

Book I: Foundations

Seven papers that establish the field and its conceptual architecture. They do not assume prior familiarity with APHS. They assume only that the reader has encountered a gap between understanding and movement (between knowing something and being able to act from it), and has found the usual explanations insufficient. The function of Book I is orientation: giving the reader a place to stand from which everything else reads more clearly.

Paper 01.01. Applied Philosophy of Human Systems: A Field Articulation names the field: what it is, where it operates, what distinguishes it from adjacent domains. It establishes the core assumptions and the posture. Readers who begin here will find the rest of the collection consistently grounded in what this paper makes visible.

Paper 01.02. What APHS Is Not (and Why That Matters) is a protective move that prevents category errors before they distort the work. APHS is not a method, not psychology, not self-help, not a belief system; understanding why each of these is not the case clarifies what the field actually is and can do. Misidentifying the field is among the most reliable ways to extract nothing from it.

Paper 01.03. Field, Orientation, and Application clarifies the structural relationship between the field and any applications developed from it. Establishes why orientation and prescription are different in kind, not in degree, and why APHS stops before application by structural necessity rather than modesty. This paper also explains the three-way independence between field, designer, and end-user that preserves the integrity of all three.

Paper 01.04. Functional Models and the Question of Truth addresses the epistemological question underlying the field: whether APHS models must be true in a metaphysical sense to be valuable. The answer, demonstrated through an extended parable of the Beneath-Dwellers, is that models serve by generating accurate patterns and enabling effective navigation, not by corresponding to ultimate reality. The miller's wheel turns regardless of whether demons pull the water down or gravitational attraction does.

Paper 01.05. Toward a Theory of Mind in APHS offers a working account of consciousness as a self-organizing system operating across multiple concurrent modes of awareness. Positioned as adjacent to the field rather than foundational: APHS does not depend on this theory, but the theory makes certain observations intelligible that would otherwise seem paradoxical. Readers whose assumptions position consciousness as the executive center will find this paper most directly useful.

Paper 01.06. Frame Shifting in APHS describes how frame-level reorganization occurs and why it cannot be forced. Distinguishes frame shifting from reframing, mindset change, and belief replacement. Establishes the other-than-conscious as the primary site of reorganization and clarifies the role conscious awareness can and cannot play in the process.

Paper 01.07. Effort, Force, and Misapplied Leverage in Human Systems locates the problem of struggle not in willpower or capacity but in where effort is being directed. Distinguishes effort from force, force from leverage, and mechanical responsiveness from systemic reorganization. This paper is where the core assumptions most directly meet the practical experience of being stuck.

Book II: Reorganization

Seven papers that demonstrate the field operating in the conditions where it is most needed: where frames no longer fit, where effort produces friction instead of movement, where the way forward requires something other than more of what has already been tried. The function of Book II is reorganization: showing how perception actually shifts and what becomes possible when it does.

Paper 02.01. Frames as Pictorial and Metaphorical Structures extends the account of frames by examining how they operate not as ideas but as pictorial and metaphorical structures. Frames are pre-verbal: rarely experienced as thoughts because they are not thoughts. This paper explains what frames actually are at the structural level, which changes how a shift in them can be recognized and why certain questions restore movement while others reinforce the existing frame.

Paper 02.02. Why Insight Often Precedes Action addresses a gap most accounts of change ignore: the interval between insight and action. Explains why the sequence is perception, then integration, then expression, and why forcing action before integration completes undermines rather than accelerates change. This paper is for readers who have had insight that did not translate into movement, and who interpreted the gap as evidence that the insight was insufficient.

Paper 02.03. Orientation Versus Optimization draws the distinction between two fundamentally different kinds of problem that are routinely conflated. Optimization refines performance within an existing frame. Orientation addresses the frame itself. When these are confused, the result is visible progress that masks invisible misalignment. Optimization not only fails to address orientation errors; it actively obscures them, reinforcing the frame's stability through visible evidence of improvement.

Paper 02.04. Translational and Transformational Change establishes the hard distinction between movement within a frame and reorganization of the frame itself. Provides language for recognizing which kind of change is occurring and responding appropriately. Neither kind is hierarchically superior. The problem arises when they are confused: when translational effort is applied to a transformational situation, anchoring the old frame in place.

Paper 02.05. Agency Without Command restores agency by relocating it from control over outcomes to coherent participation in systems that organize through meaning rather than force. Examines leadership as an emergent expression of this form of agency. Agency does not require command. When someone stands clearly, participates coherently, and allows systems to organize around their clarity, movement often follows, and that movement is real capacity, not compliance.

Paper 02.06. Choice as a System Property clarifies choice as a constant property of self-organizing systems rather than a capacity that appears and disappears based on willpower. Human systems are always choosing. What varies is whether they have access to resourceful options. Explains why protective choosing is accurate rather than avoidant, how resourceful options expand when conditions support them, and why forcing commitment when protective choosing is operative produces decisions the system cannot sustain.

Paper 02.07. A Thought Experiment in Orientation and Navigation ties the preceding work together through an extended thought experiment, demonstrating how the field's observations function in an integrated navigational context. An imagined being learns to navigate constraints, discover what works through feedback, and reorganize orientation when existing approaches no longer produce movement.

Book III: Integration

Seven papers that address a different and easily missed risk: not the original problem of stuckness, but the secondary problem that arrives after movement resumes. The impulse to convert new orientation into a system. To close what needs to remain open. To turn living understanding into something that can be managed. The function of Book III is integration: supporting the reader in remaining with reorganization without forcing closure. The risk it addresses is not getting stuck again but converting new orientation into a system to manage, which produces the very brittleness the work was designed to dissolve.

Paper 03.01. How to Read This Work Without Turning It Into a System comes first because it addresses the reader's instinct before the reader acts on it. By the time someone reaches Book III, enough material has accumulated that the pull toward systemization is strong. This paper explains why converting this work into a system collapses what it is designed to do, and clarifies reading for alignment as the appropriate mode of engagement.

Paper 03.02. Where You're Probably Standing Right Now meets the reader where they are likely to actually be standing: uncertain, between positions, unclear whether what is happening is progress or drift. Describes common vantage points without ranking them. The function is recognition rather than instruction: knowing where you are standing so that what is visible from there can be engaged directly rather than from where you imagine you should be.

Paper 03.03. Holding a New Frame During Reorganization addresses the specific challenge of holding a new frame before it has stabilized: before the systems embedded in the reader's life have adjusted to it, before it has become ordinary. Distinguishes holding from gripping, and explains why effort applied at this stage (vigilance, enforcement, deliberate maintenance) produces the reversion it is trying to prevent.

Paper 03.04. Continuity, Momentum, and Perceived Stuckness examines the interpretive error that reads invisible integration as stagnation: the loss of familiar feedback that the mind fills with the conclusion that nothing is moving. Works against the impulse to intervene in a process that is proceeding correctly by explaining what invisible integration actually looks like and what it indicates.

Paper 03.05. What It Looks Like When Nothing Seems to Be Happening describes the integration interval from the inside: not dramatic, not obviously meaningful, not clearly pointing anywhere. Complements 03.04 by attending to the texture of the experience rather than the interpretive error about it. This paper is for readers who are in that interval and need to recognize it for what it is.

Paper 03.06. What Changed While You Weren't Looking addresses the experience of retrospective discovery: arriving somewhere and noticing that you have already been different for a while without being aware of it. Examines why most integration proceeds invisibly and what that retrospective recognition reveals about how the process was working during the interval when it appeared not to be.

Paper 03.07. Leaving the Frame Open closes the volume and the collection. Addresses the mind's impulse to close the frame: to convert the work into finished understanding that can be summarized, retained, and explained. Makes the case that this closure, though natural, eliminates the condition under which the work continues to function. What the reader is being asked to leave open is not unfinished. It is complete in a sense that requires remaining open.

. . .

5. What the Full Picture Offers

A grasp of APHS in full (its assumptions, vocabulary, domains, and arc) is not a technique and does not produce a method. What it produces is a different quality of seeing. That shift in what becomes visible has practical consequences that vary depending on who is engaging the field. Three genuinely distinct uses emerge.

For Someone Navigating Their Own Life

APHS provides a different way of interpreting experience, particularly when effort is not producing movement. Instead of concluding that something is wrong with you, you have vocabulary and distinctions that let you ask a more useful question: where am I standing, and does that position allow movement? That reframe relocates the problem from character to structure, which is almost always more addressable.

What becomes visible: the frame you are inside, the orientation you are working from, whether your effort is translational when the situation requires transformation, whether you are applying force where coherence is what is actually needed. None of this is technique. These are perceptual shifts: changes in what you notice and how you interpret what you see. But those shifts have practical consequences, because action that follows from accurate orientation requires less force and produces more sustainable movement.

Concretely: a person with a full grasp of APHS can recognize when they are in a frame that no longer fits, rather than intensifying effort within it. They can distinguish between genuine stuckness and the quiet interval of integration that looks like stuckness from the outside. They can stop interpreting protective choosing as failure of will and start reading it as structural information. They can recognize when insight has already occurred at the frame level before behavior has caught up, and stop forcing premature action that would collapse the reorganization. They can hold a new frame without gripping it during the vulnerable period before it stabilizes. They can allow change to proceed at the timing the system requires rather than at the timing pressure demands.

For Someone Who Builds Frameworks or Practices

APHS provides something that application-level training rarely offers: a coherent understanding of the dynamics your tools are working with and working against. When a technique stops producing results, APHS gives a principled place to look. Is the frame misaligned? Is translational effort being applied to a transformational situation? Is the tool creating conditions, or attempting to force outcomes? Is agency being preserved or suppressed?

A designer who understands APHS builds differently from the start: for self-organization rather than compliance, for conditions rather than behaviors, for preserved agency rather than managed dependency. They can locate their application's proper scope: knowing what it can and cannot do, and where the field-level work ends and their own application-level accountability begins. APHS does not authorize or govern downstream applications. But its observations, inhabited honestly, produce better-designed applications than those built without that orientation, because the designer knows what they are actually working with.

The field also protects designers from a specific failure mode: the collapse of a method when the designer cannot explain its own failure. When techniques stop working, designers without APHS orientation tend to either refine the technique (applying more of what is not working) or abandon it (concluding it was wrong). A designer who understands the underlying dynamics can ask a more useful question: what level is the problem operating at, and is my tool designed to reach that level?

For Someone Who Has Exhausted Application-Level Work

Someone who has tried every available method and still finds that something essential has not shifted has likely been addressing symptoms rather than the interpretive structure beneath them. Not because the applications failed, but because what needed to change was operating at a level applications do not reach. This is not a criticism of the applications. APHS itself is explicit that applications serve their own function, and that function is not the same as the field's.

For that person, APHS offers clarity about the dynamics beneath the methods. Not another method, but visibility into why the methods were not reaching the right level. That clarity itself, without any further technique, sometimes restores movement that months or years of effort could not, because it shifts the frame through which the situation was being organized. The change is perceptual before it is behavioral. The reorganization precedes the explanation.

This use also identifies something important about when APHS is most appropriate as a direct engagement. For someone seeking immediate practical support, downstream applications will often serve more directly than the field itself, and APHS is explicit about this. The field is designed for those who need to understand the dynamics beneath the methods, not as a first resort for everyone navigating difficulty.

What All Three Share

In each case, what APHS provides is the same thing: a change in what becomes visible. Not instructions about what to do with what you see; that remains the person's own determination. But a different quality of seeing. Constraints that were invisible become apparent. Options that seemed unavailable reveal themselves. Problems that felt personal reveal themselves as structural. Effort that seemed necessary reveals itself as mislocated.

APHS shifts conditions by making structure visible. What happens next is the system's own response, arising from its own coherence. That response, when perception has genuinely reorganized, is typically quieter, more proportionate, and more sustainable than what force could produce. But it is also, in the field's view, more real.

...

6. Stepping Aside

This monograph has done what it set out to do: map the terrain before the reader enters it. The four dimensions (assumptions, vocabulary, domains, arc) are now in view as a whole. What each one looks like in full, what it is made of, how it relates to the others.

The founding papers will go slower. They will go deeper. Individual papers will hold at length what this overview moved through quickly. That is as it should be. The map is not the territory. This orientation is not a substitute for the work itself.

Nothing in this monograph requires adoption in order to have been useful. If a distinction clarified something in the course of reading, it has already served. If it raised a question that the founding papers will address, it has already served. If it provided enough structural orientation that the papers, when encountered directly, land with more precision, it has served.

The work can be set down at any time without loss. There is no accumulation to preserve, no progress to maintain, no framework to complete. What orients, orients. What does not can be set aside. The field does not require loyalty. It asks only that its observations be tested in experience, and retained or discarded based on whether they clarify.

Notes